Coloring book for adults and kids beautiful cupcake image for design

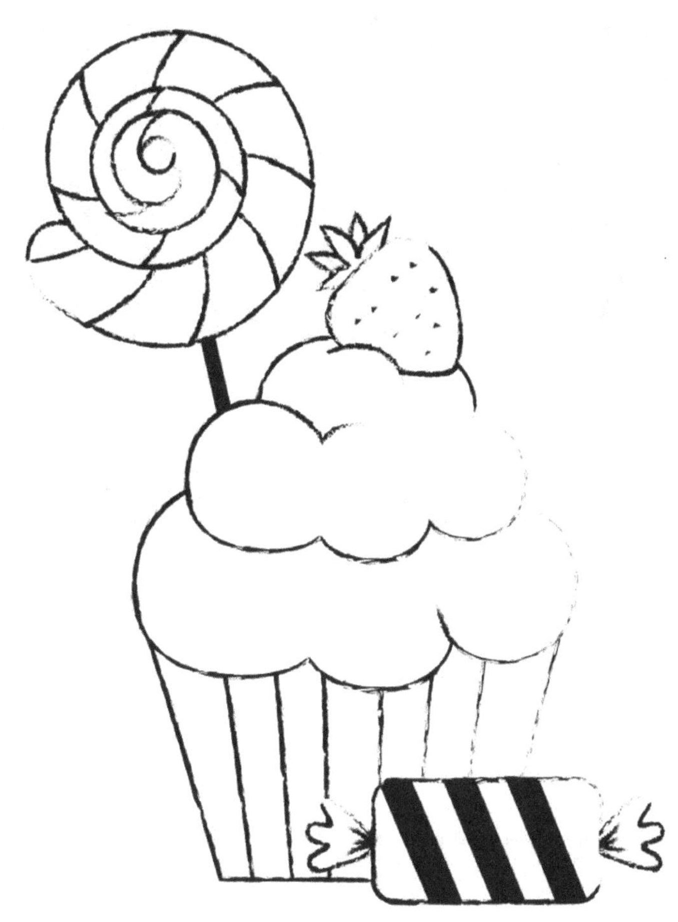

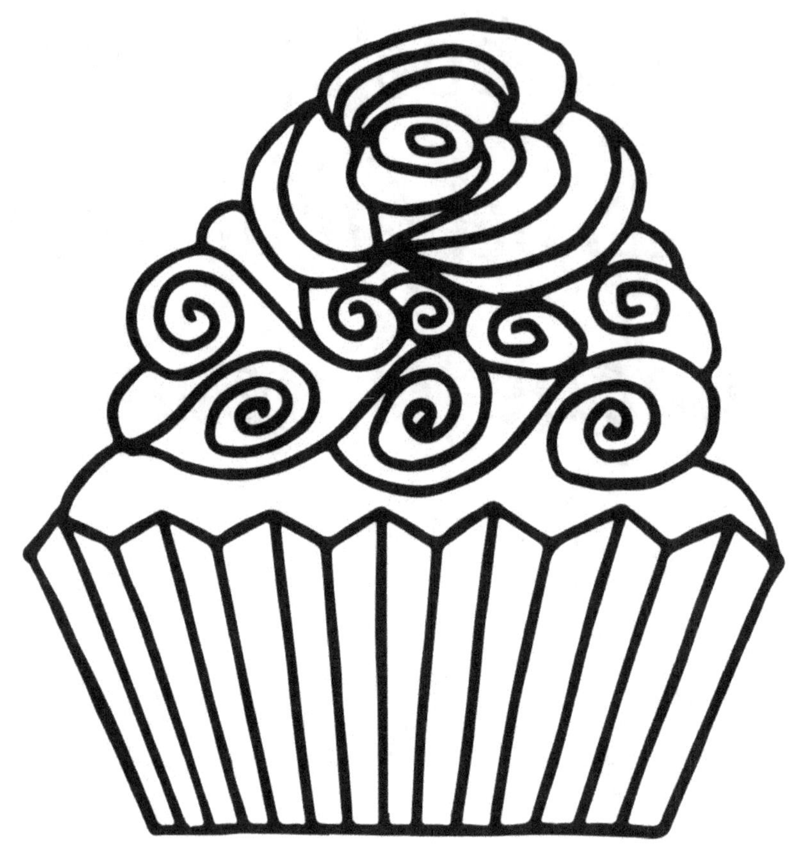

This coloring book is
belongs to

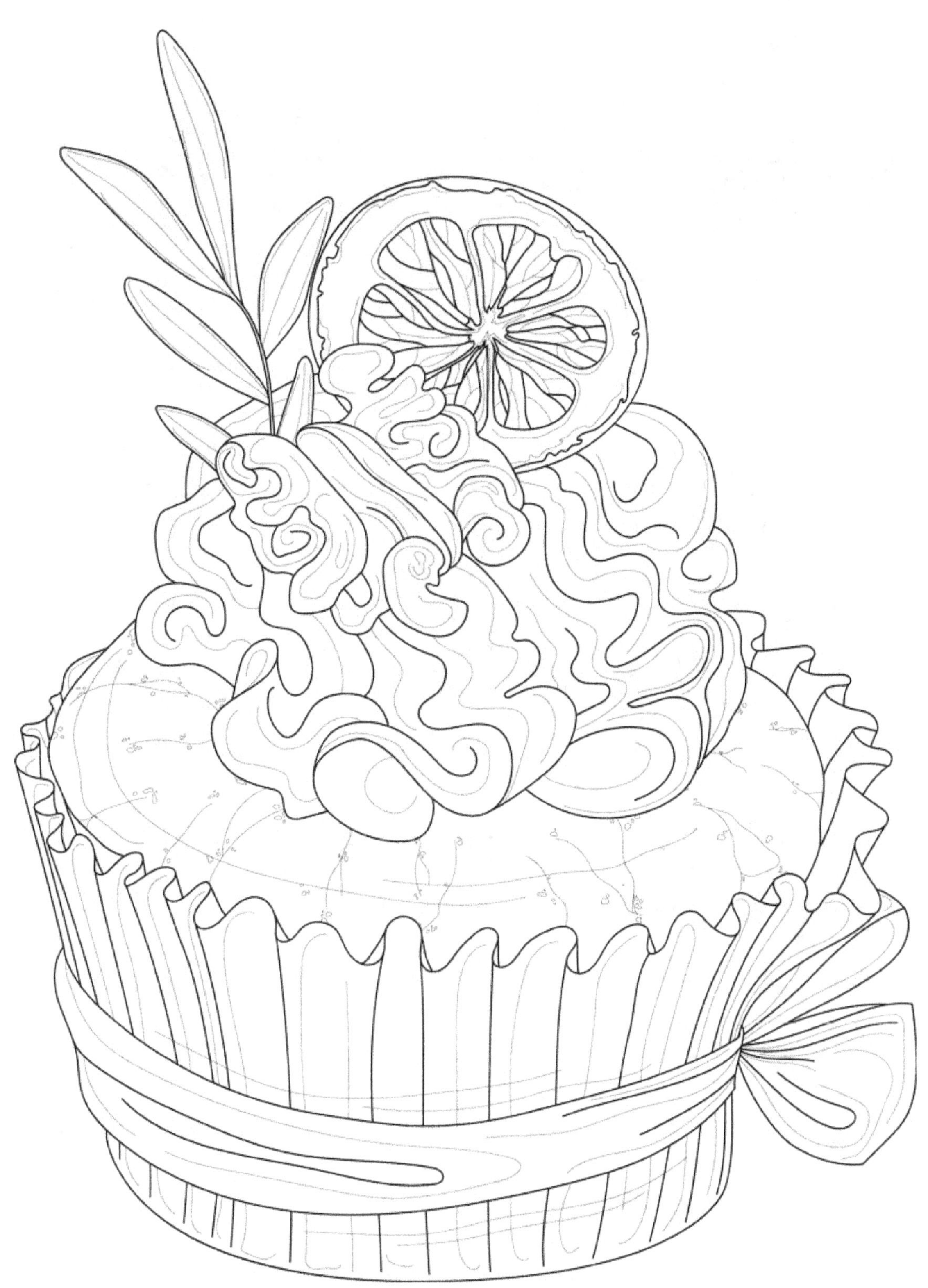

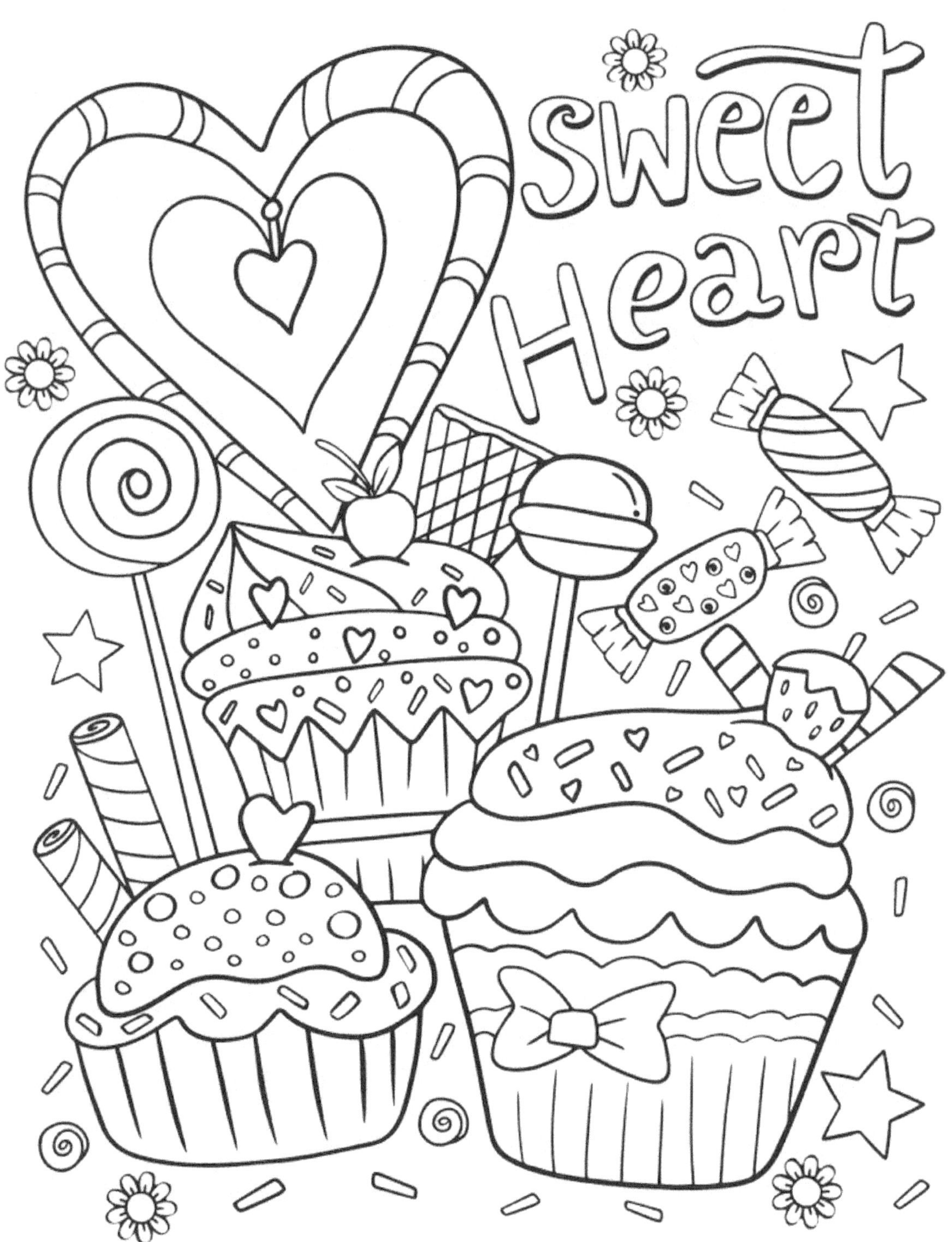

sweet
Heart

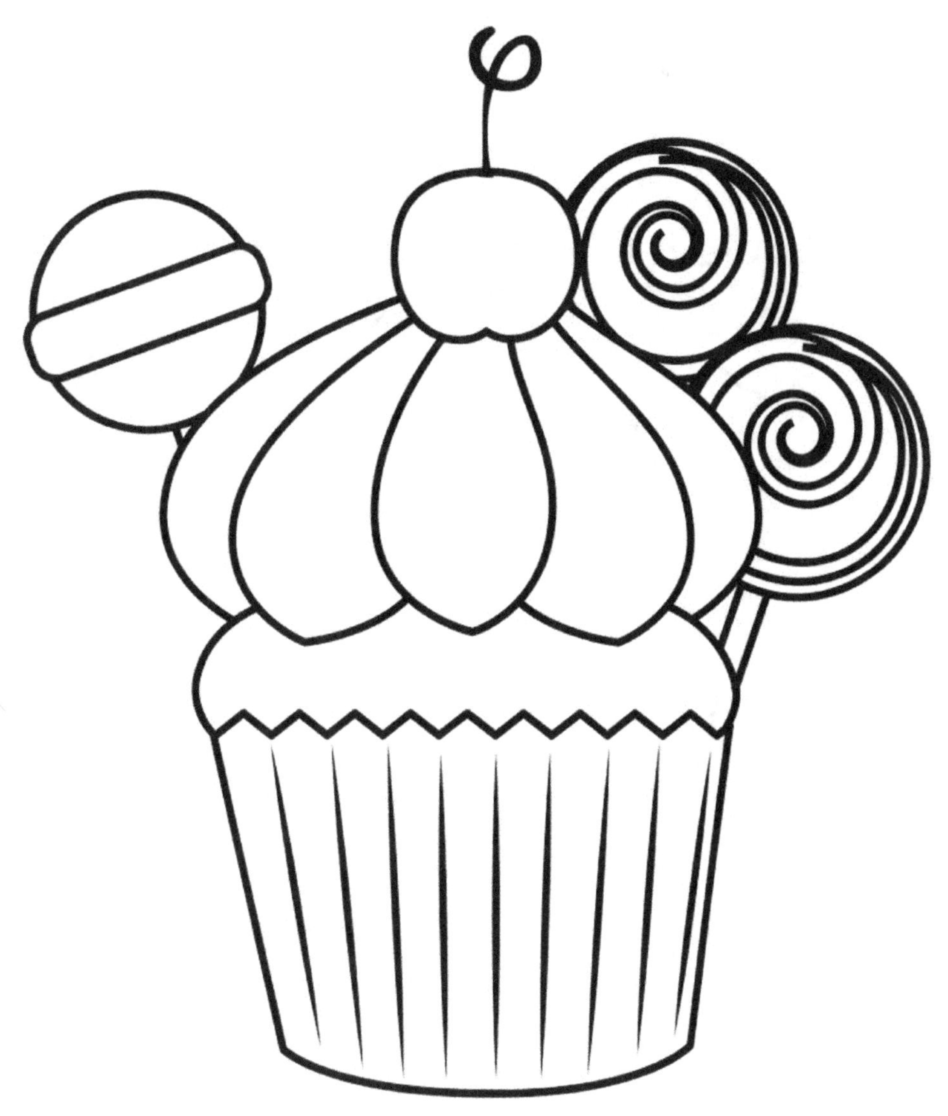

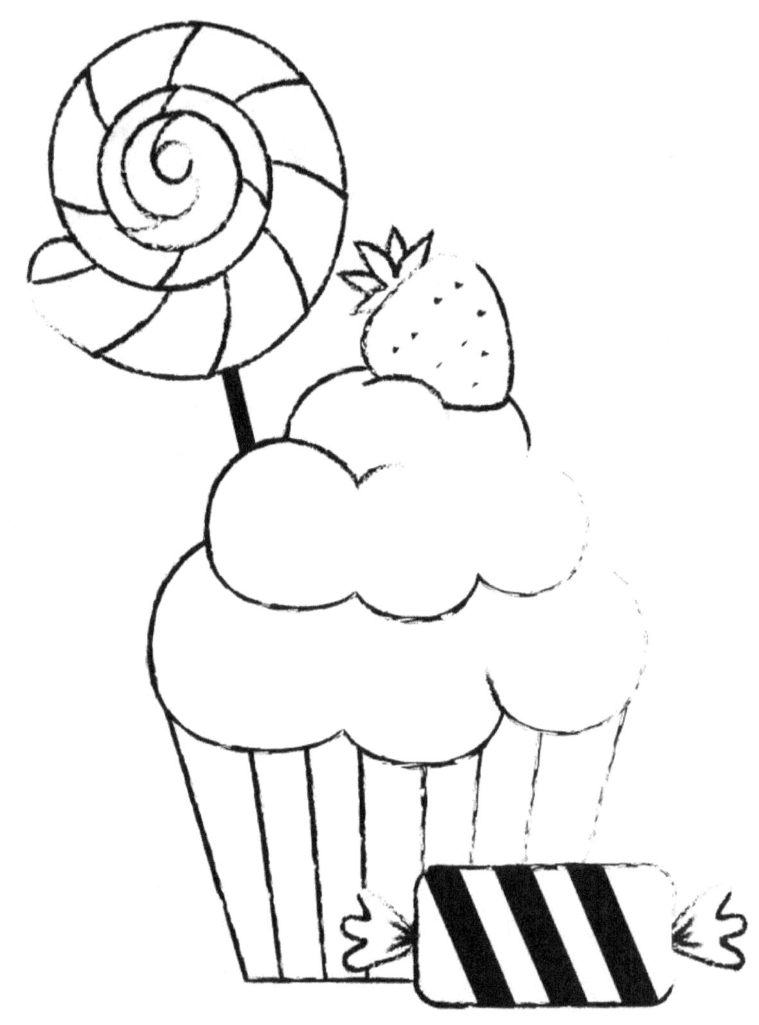

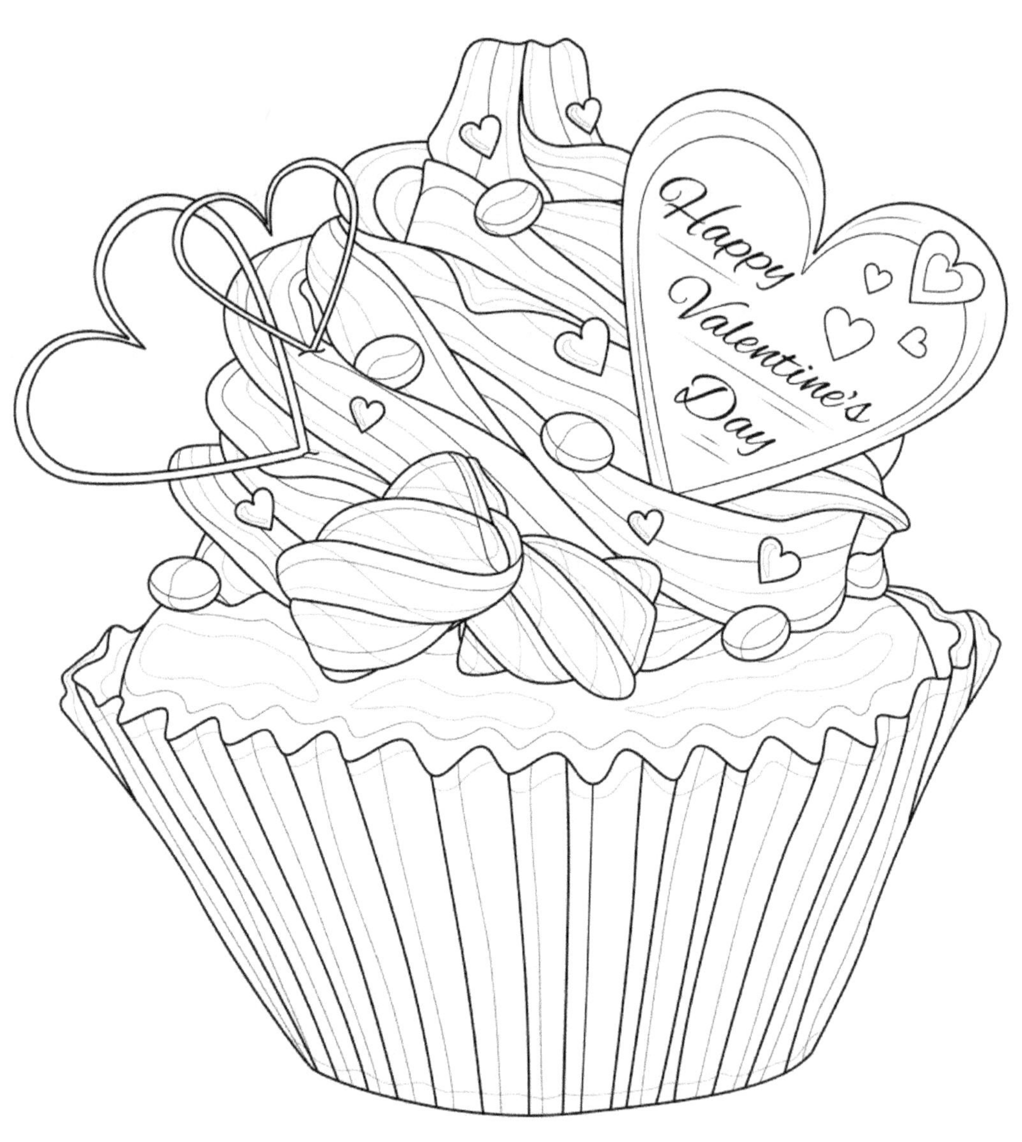
Happy
Valentine's
Day

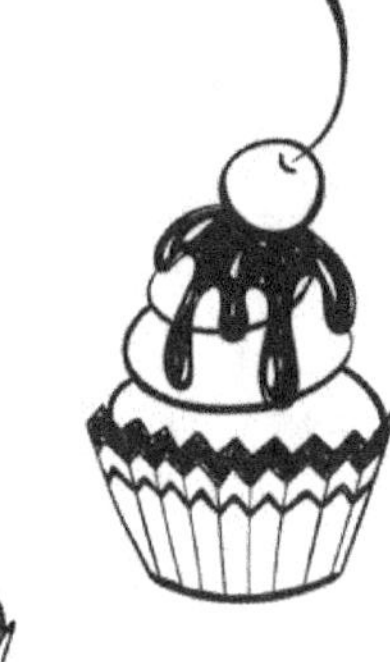
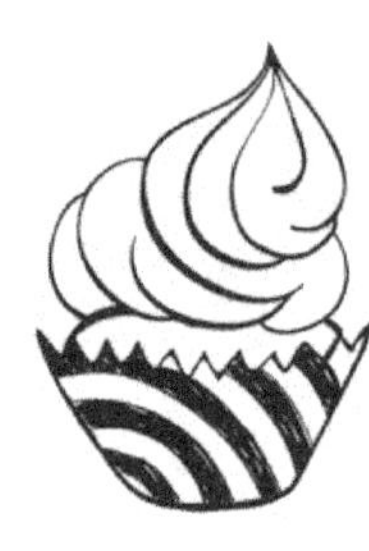
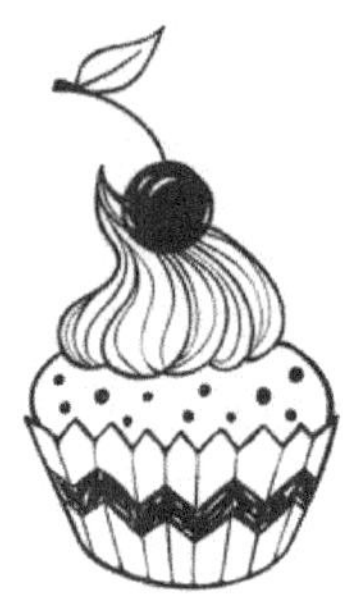
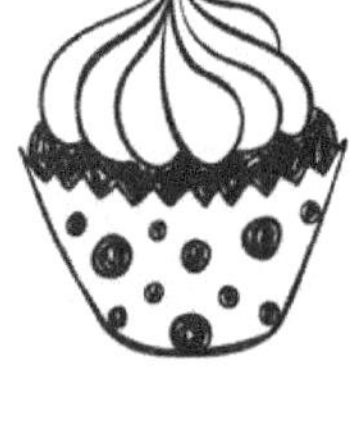
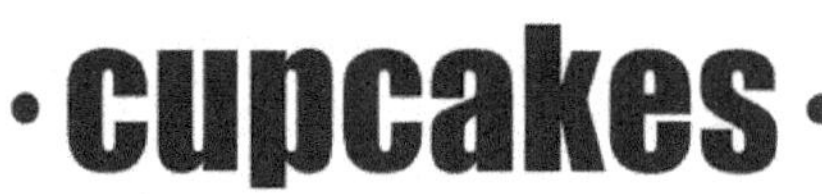
· cupcakes ·
hand drawn set
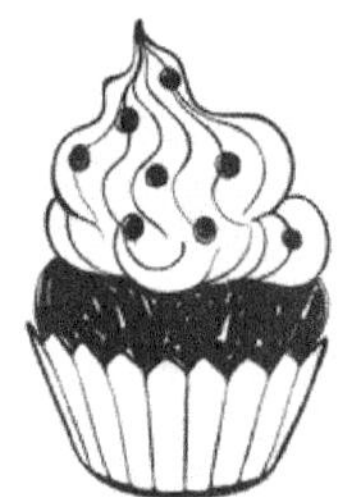
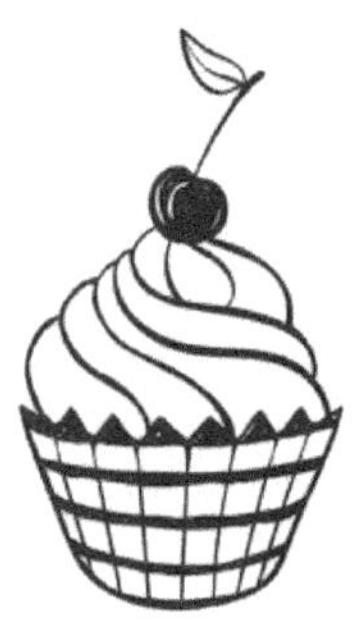
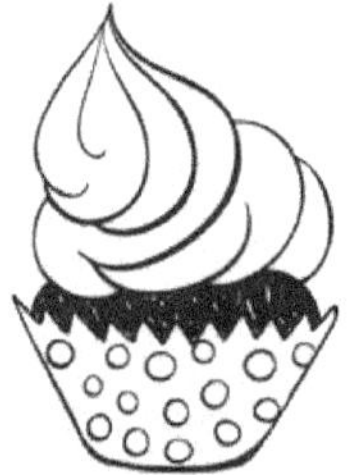
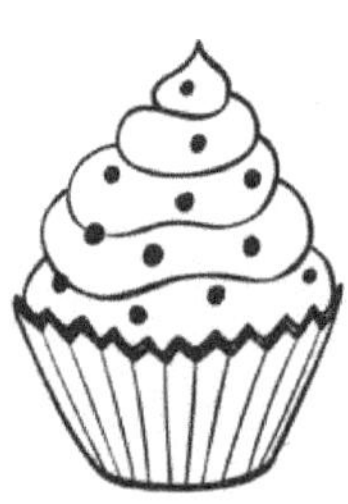
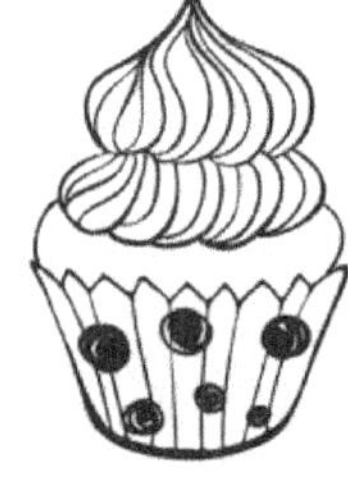

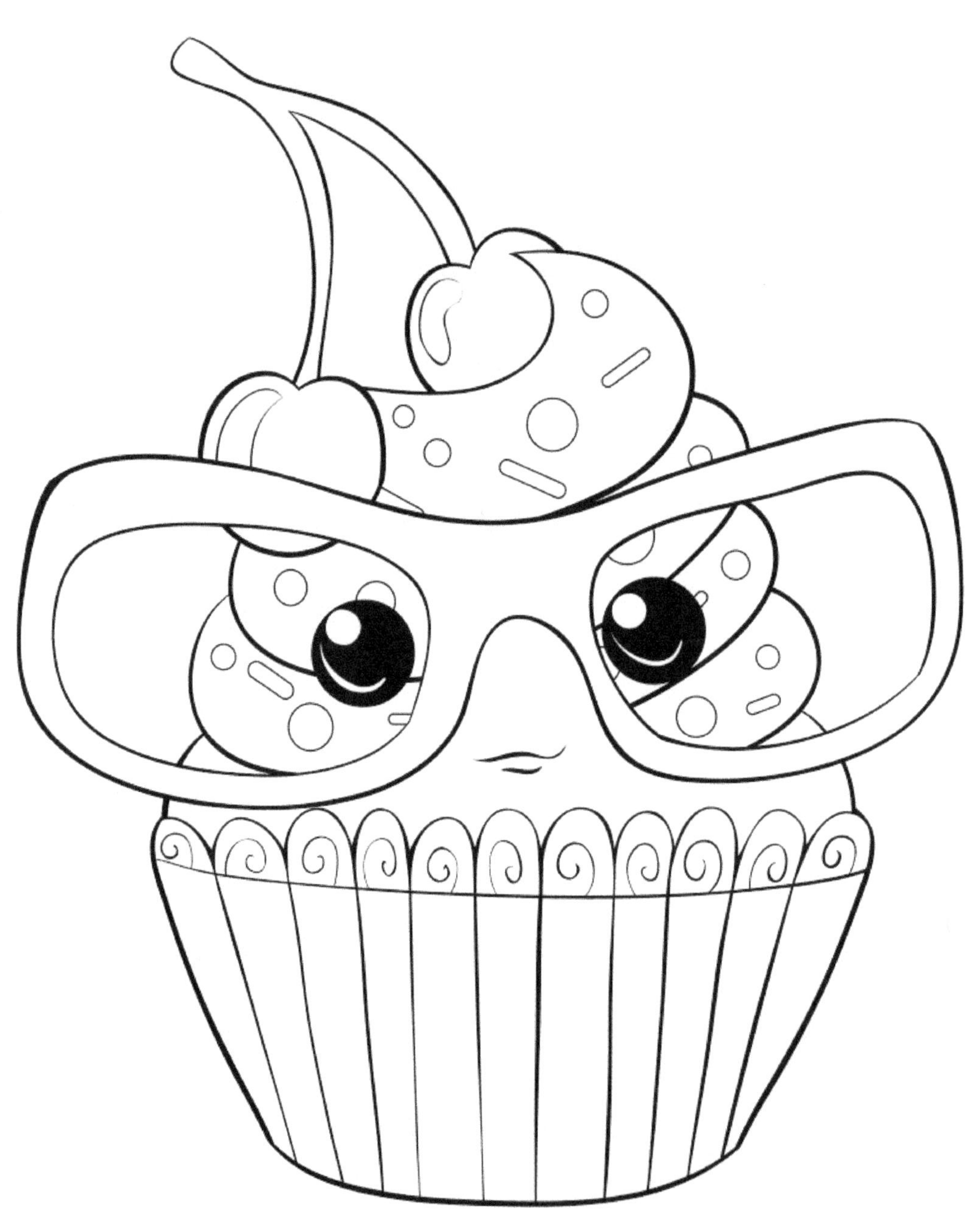

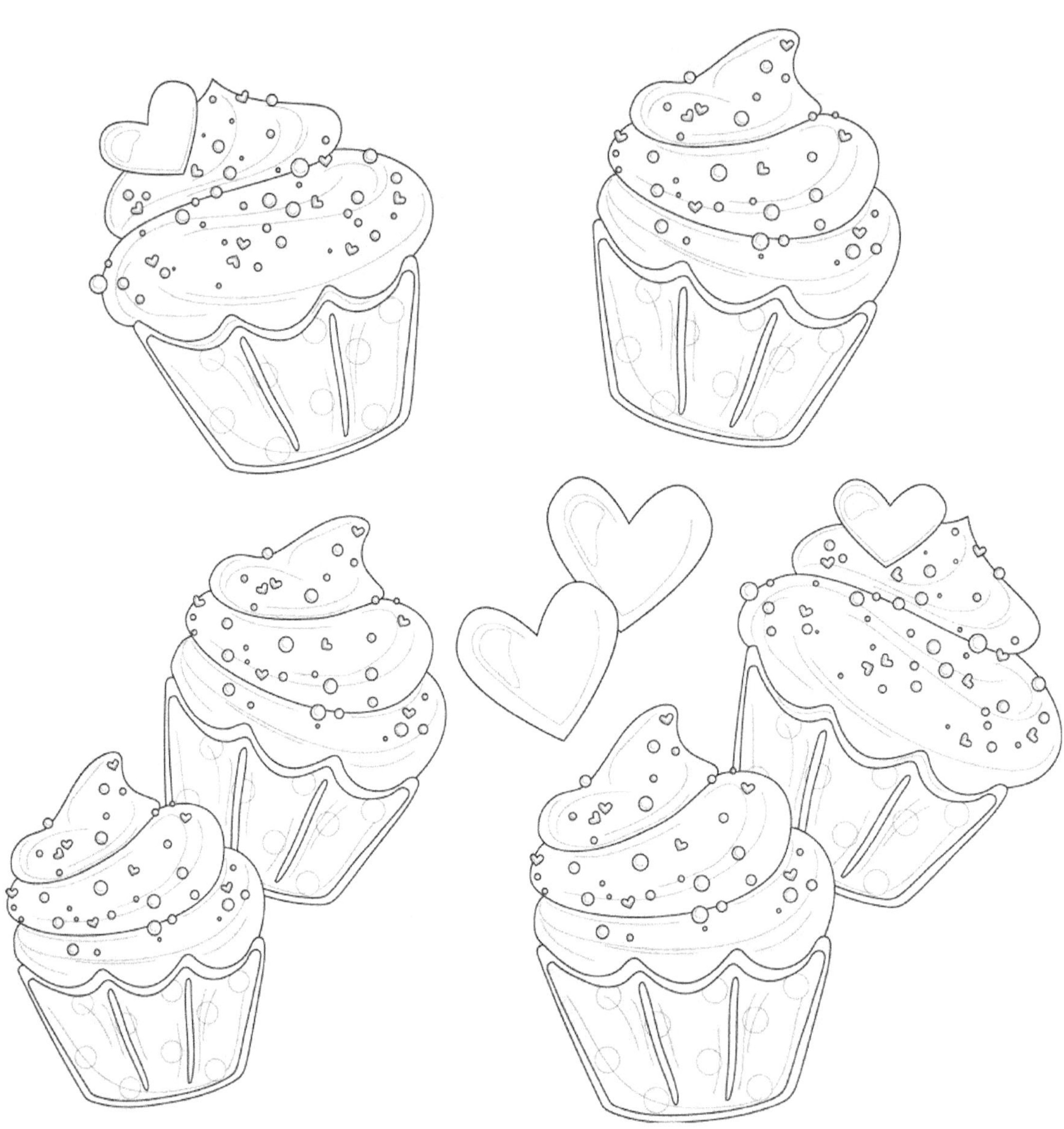

cake

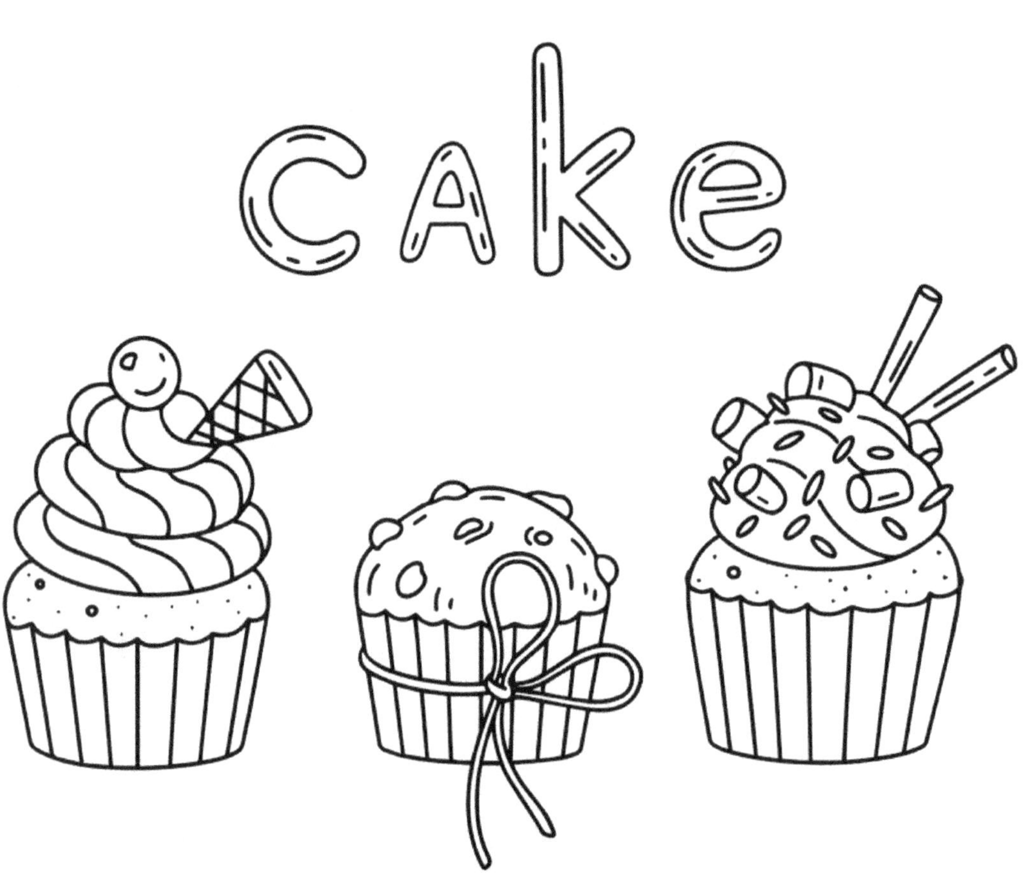

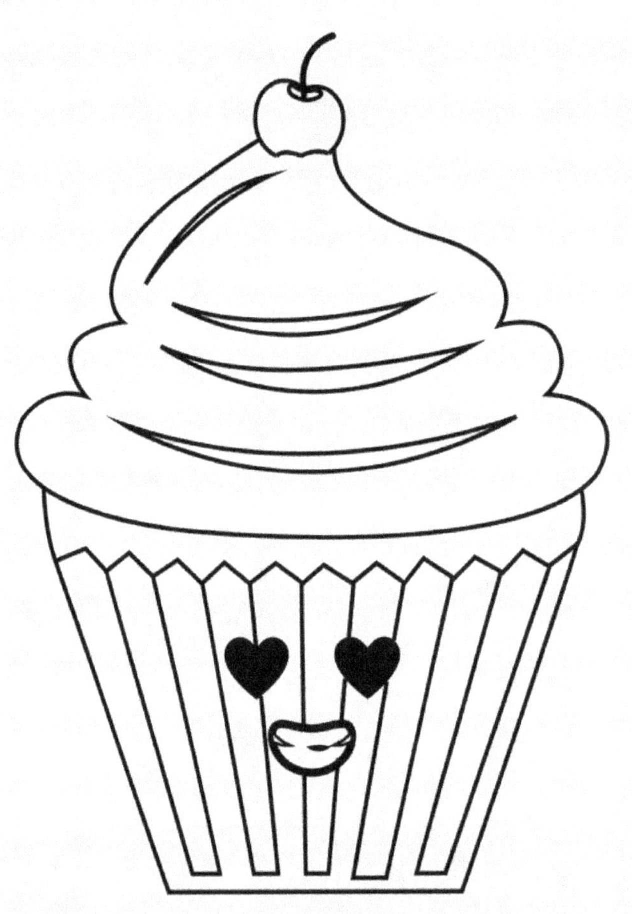

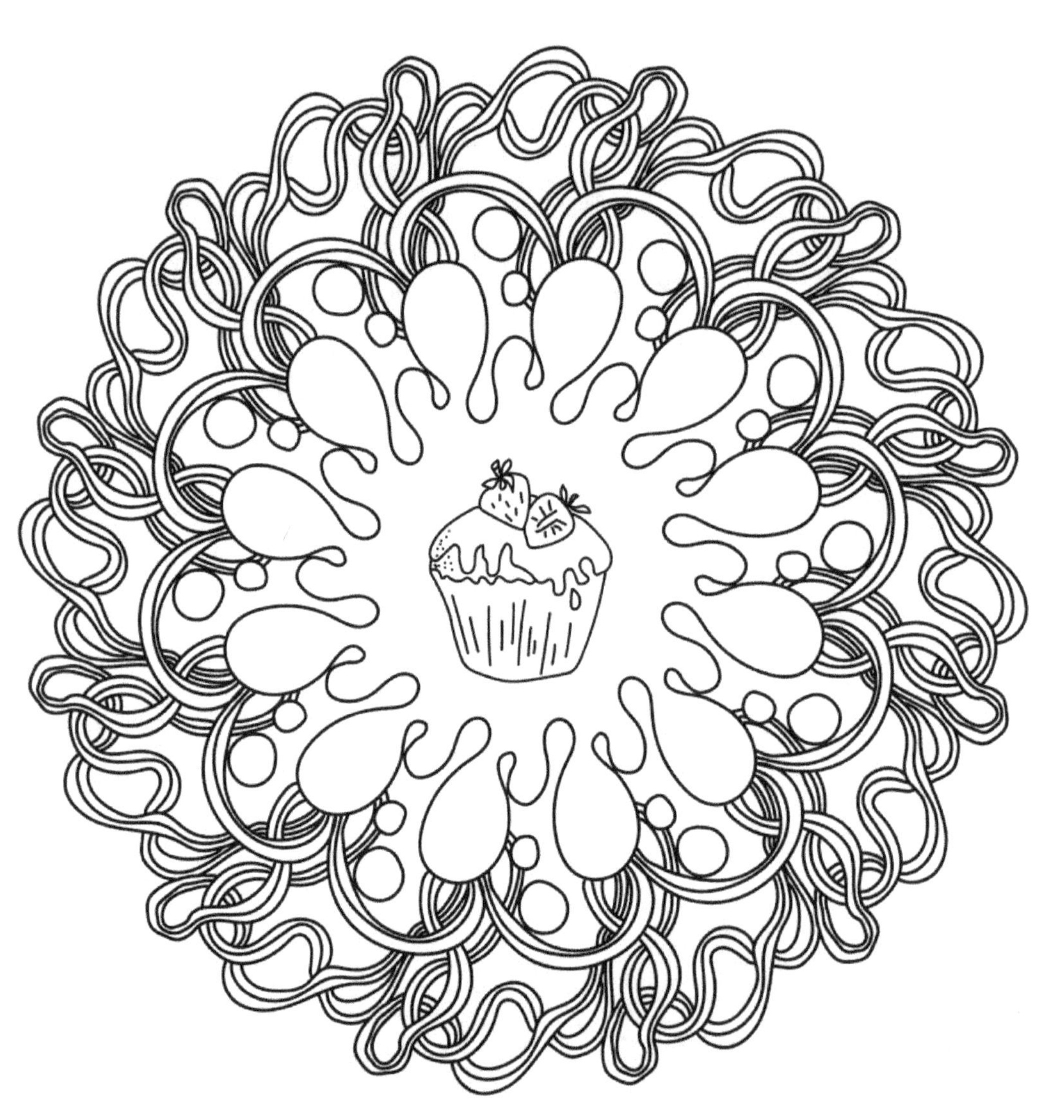

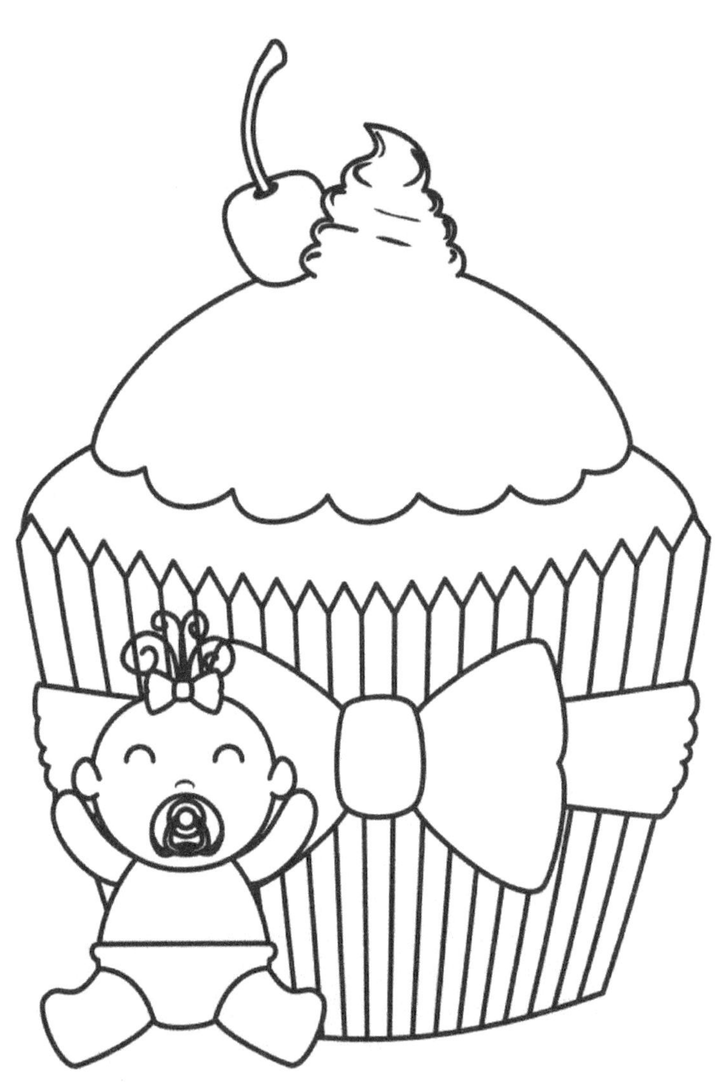

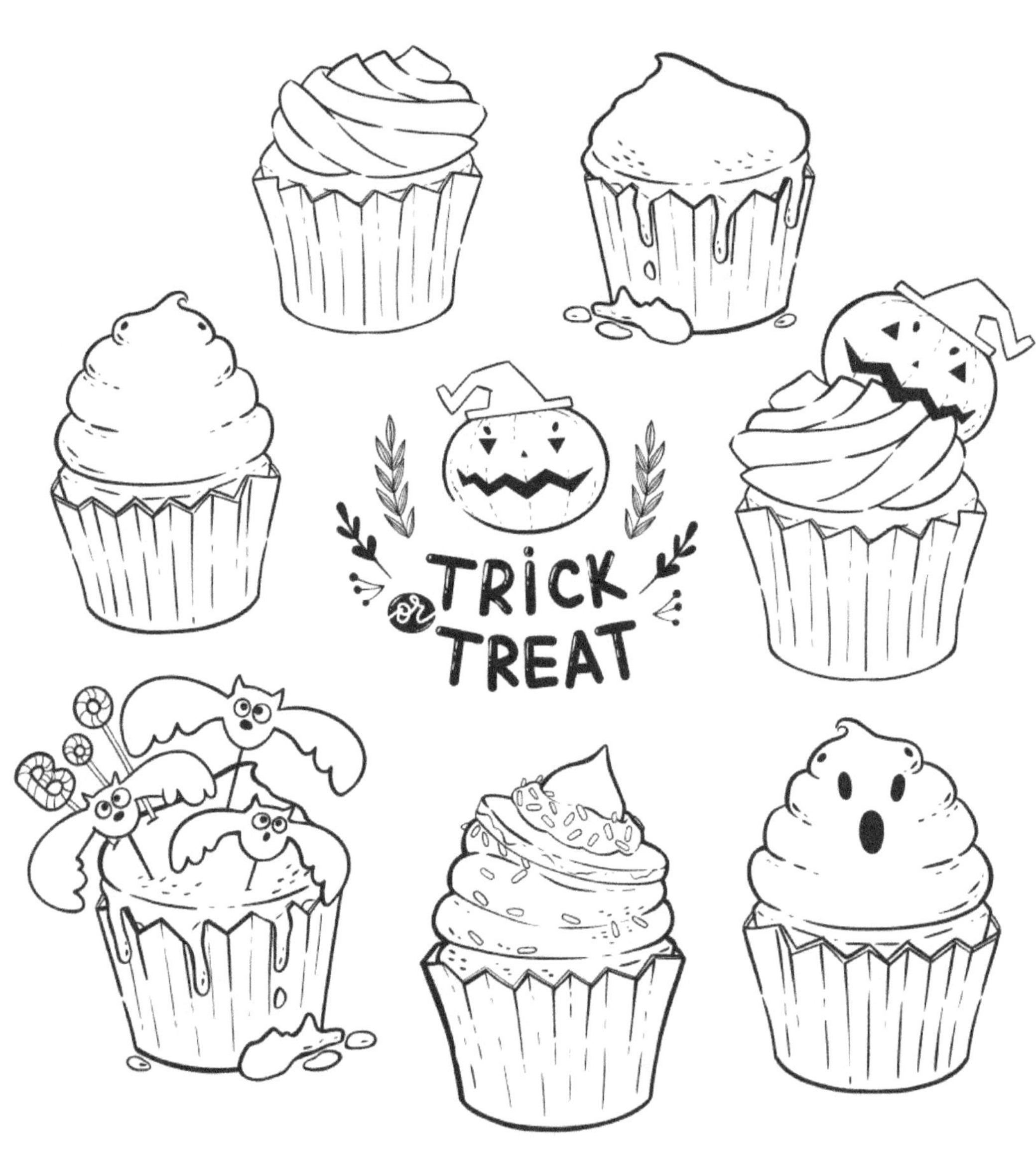
TRICK
or
TREAT

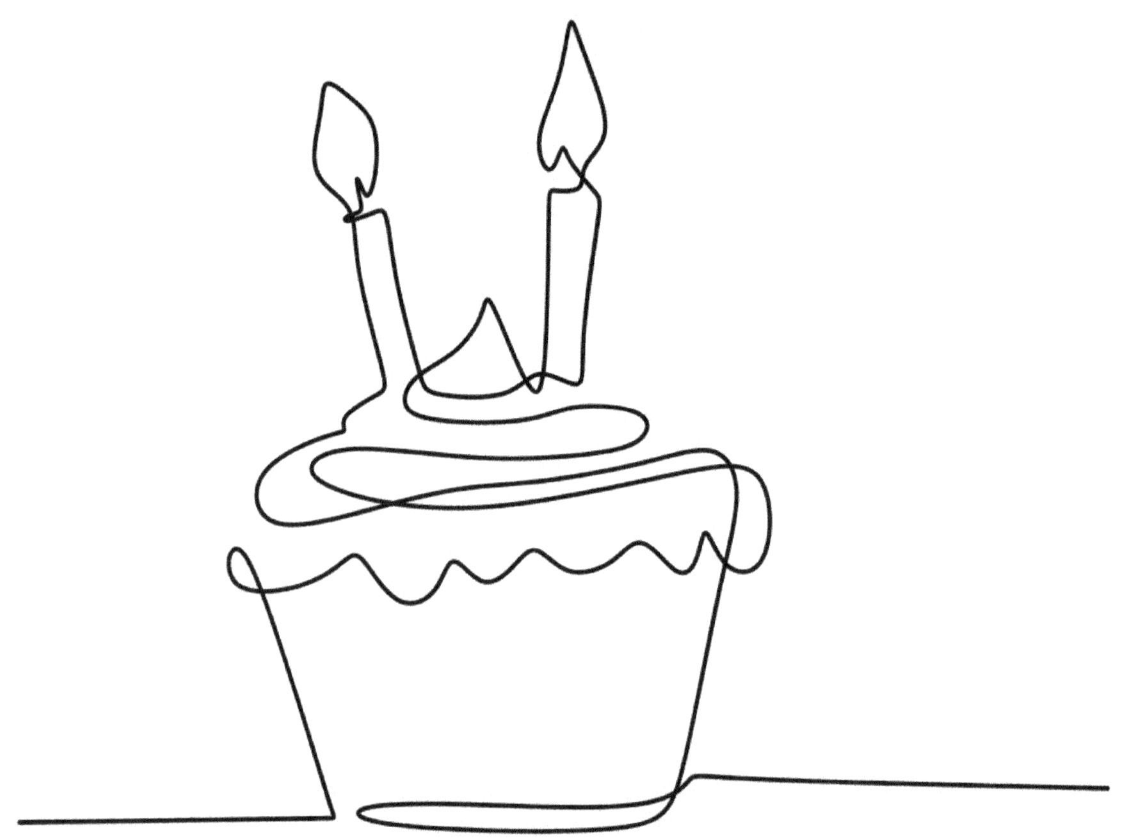

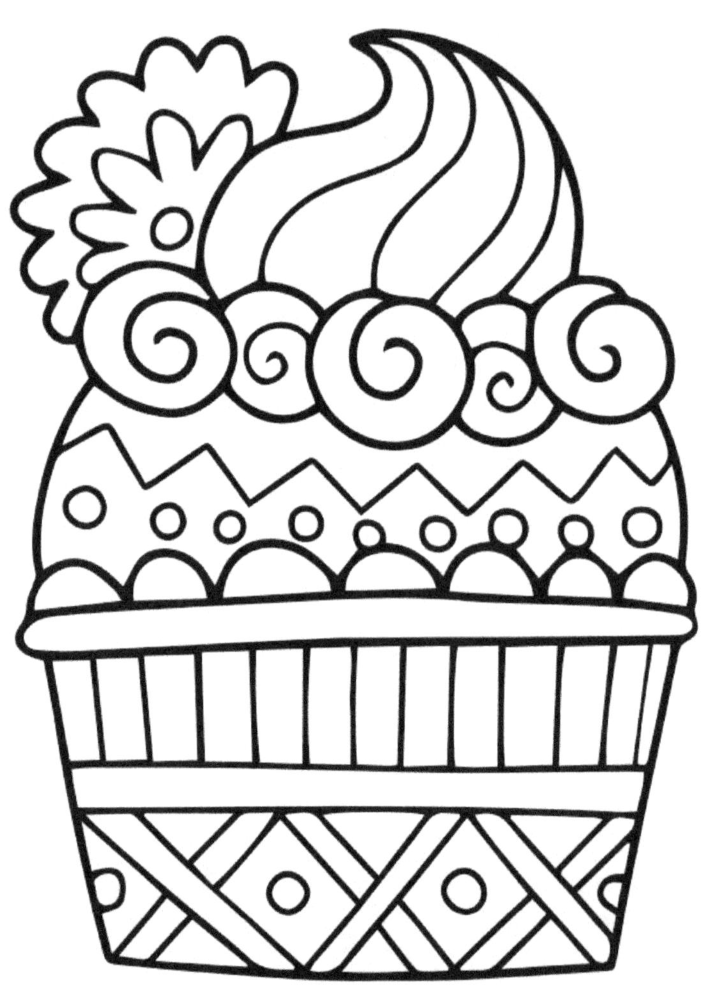

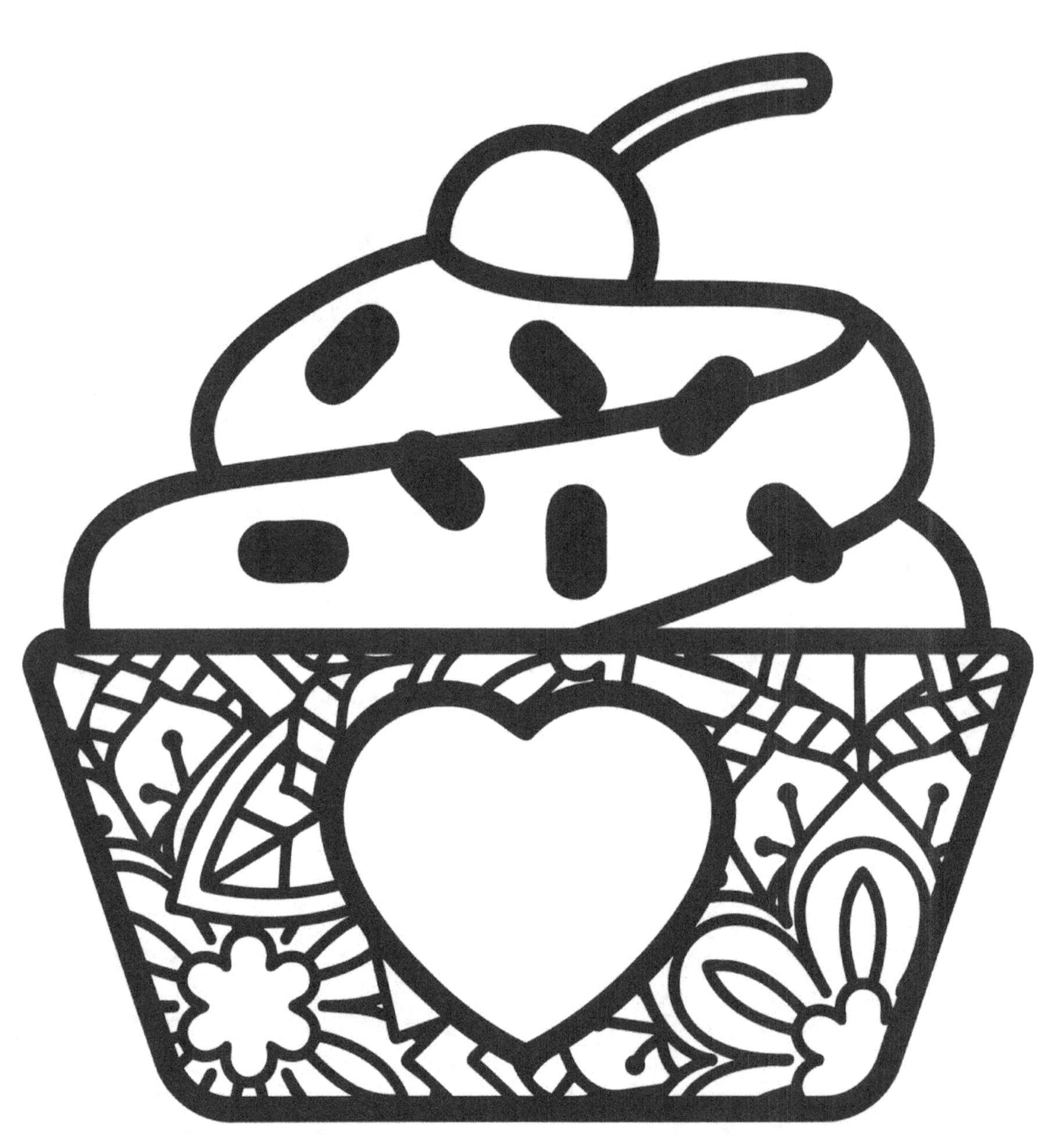

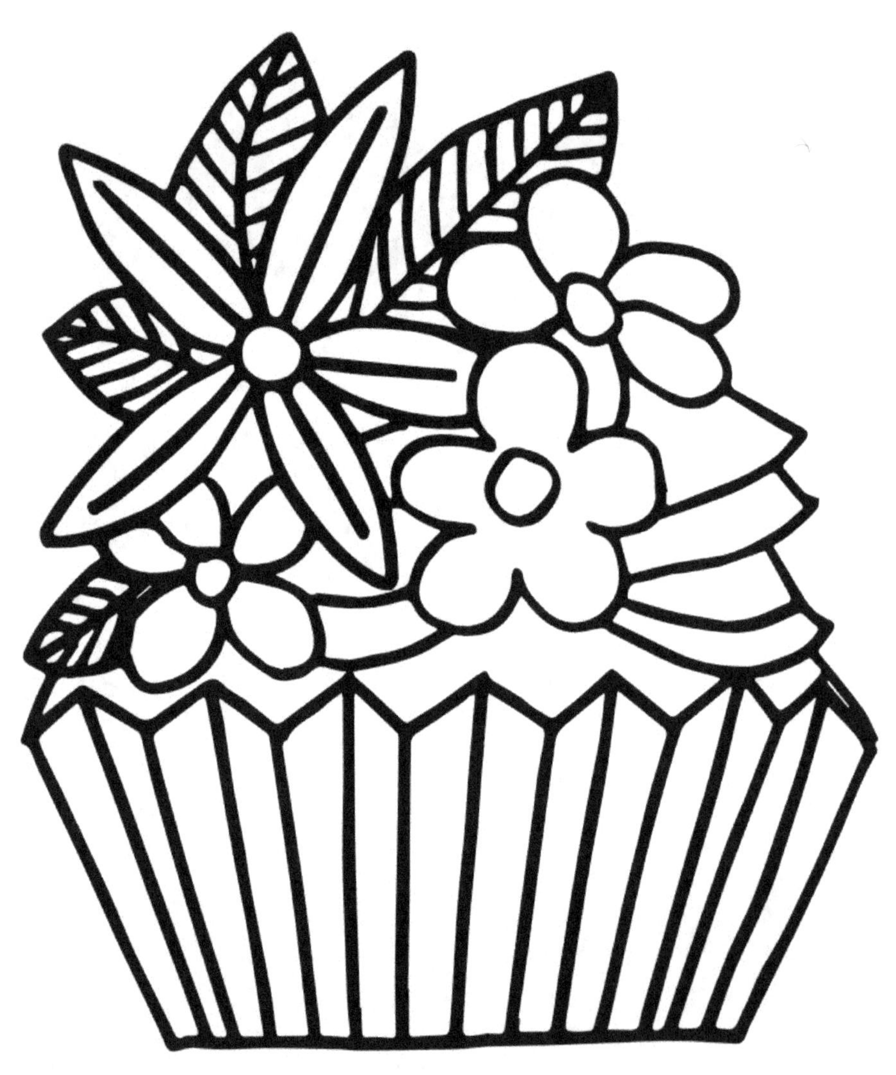

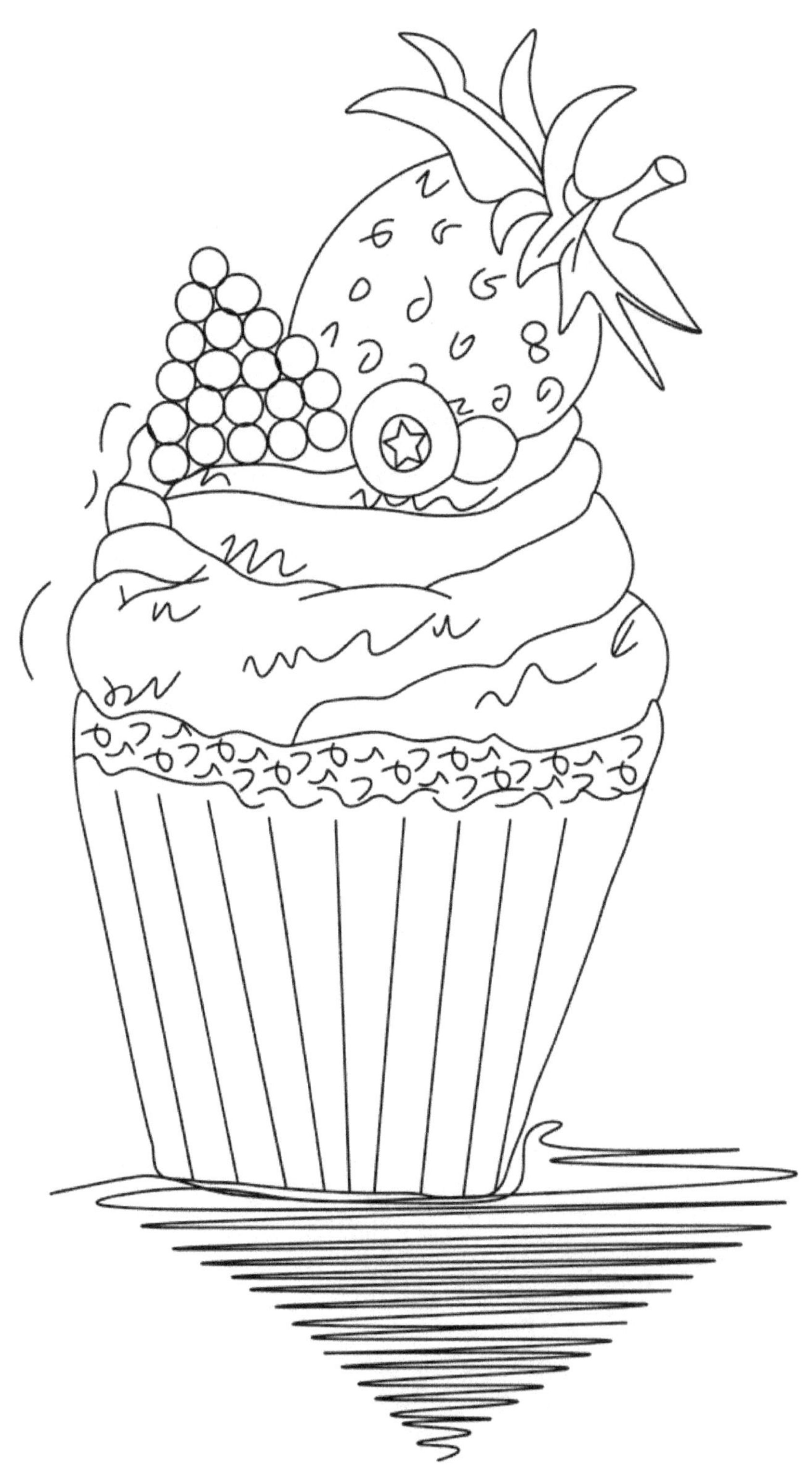

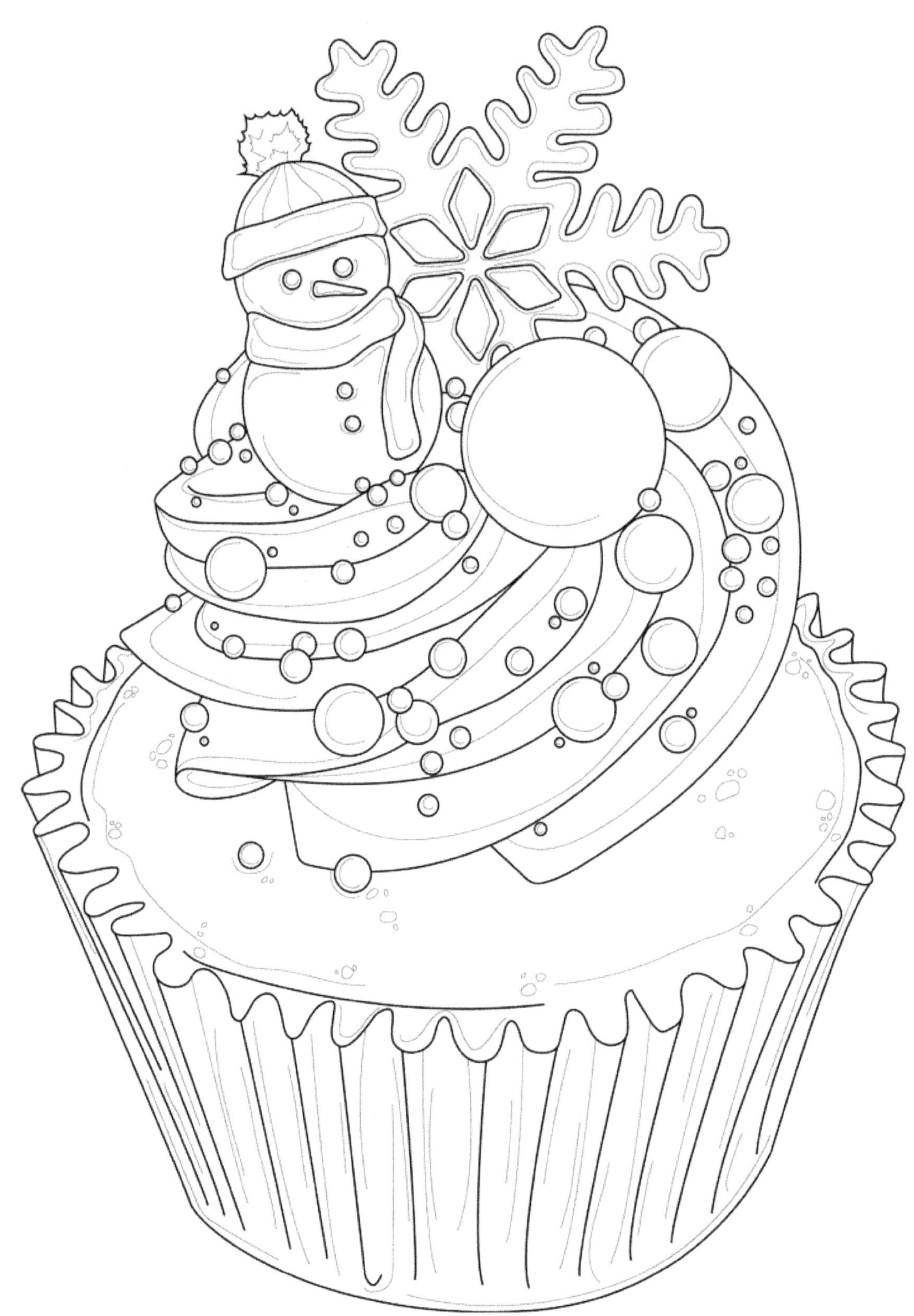

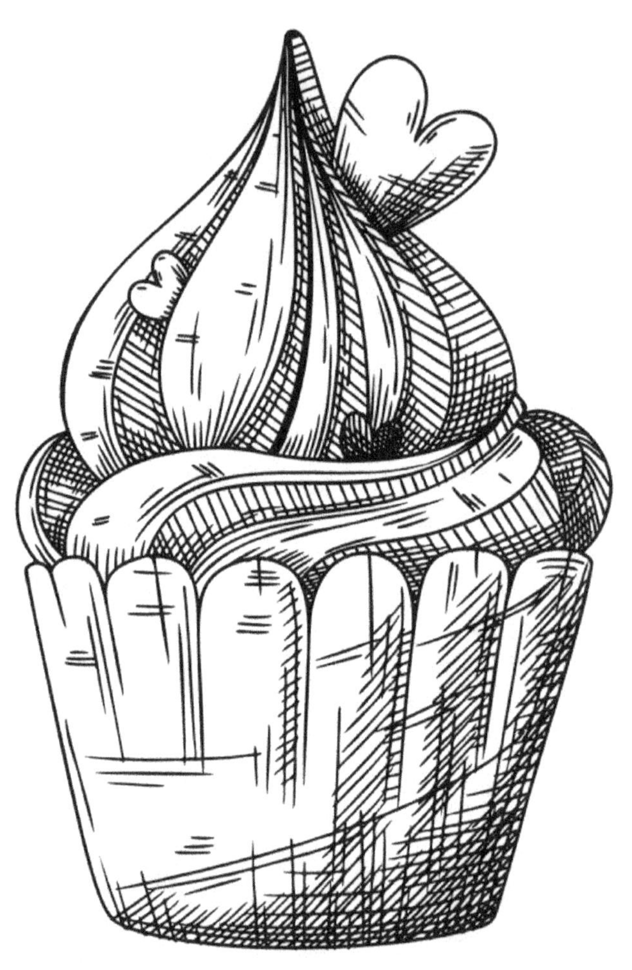

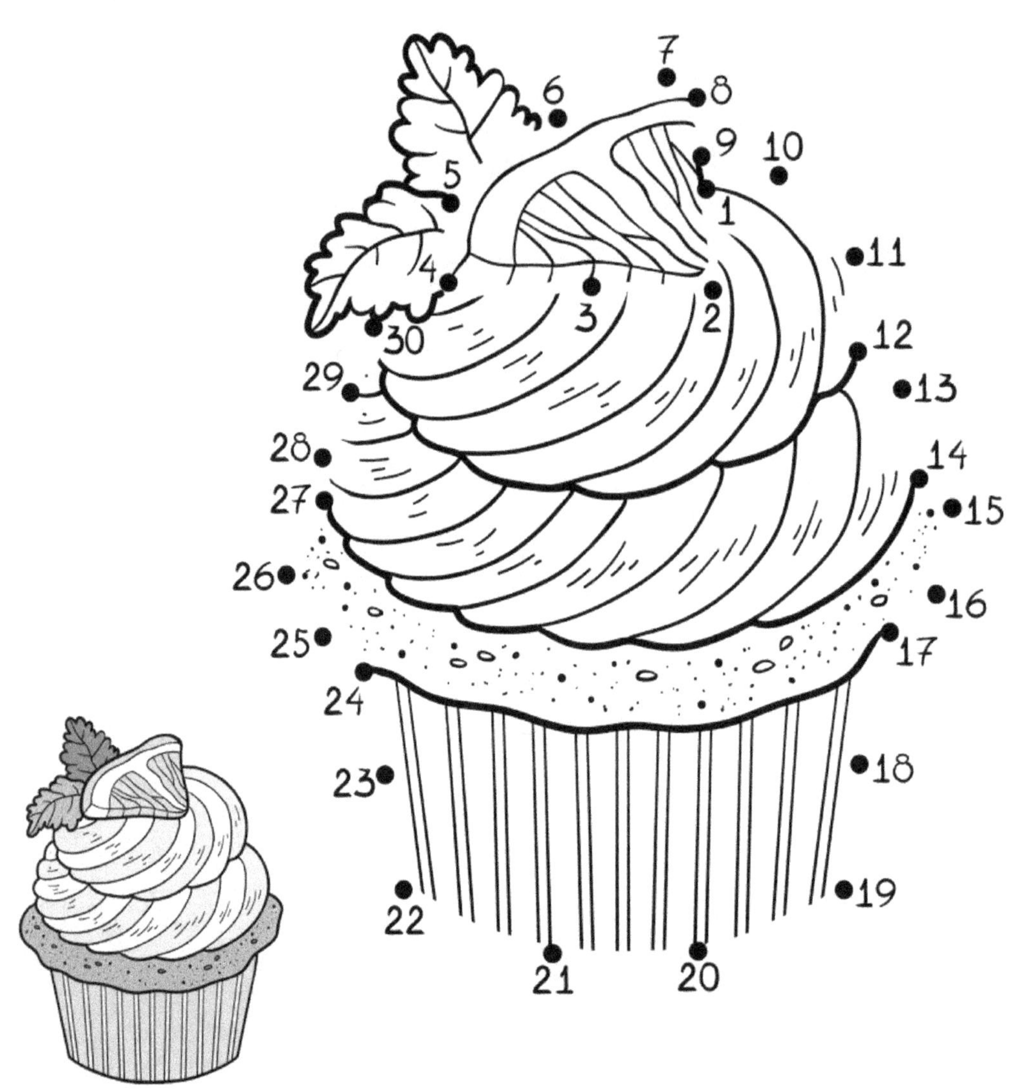

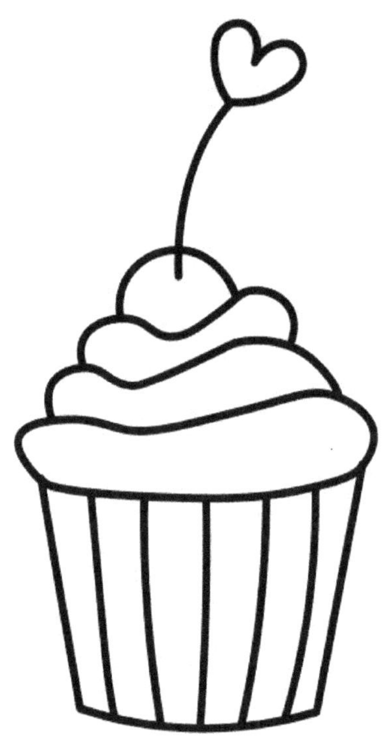

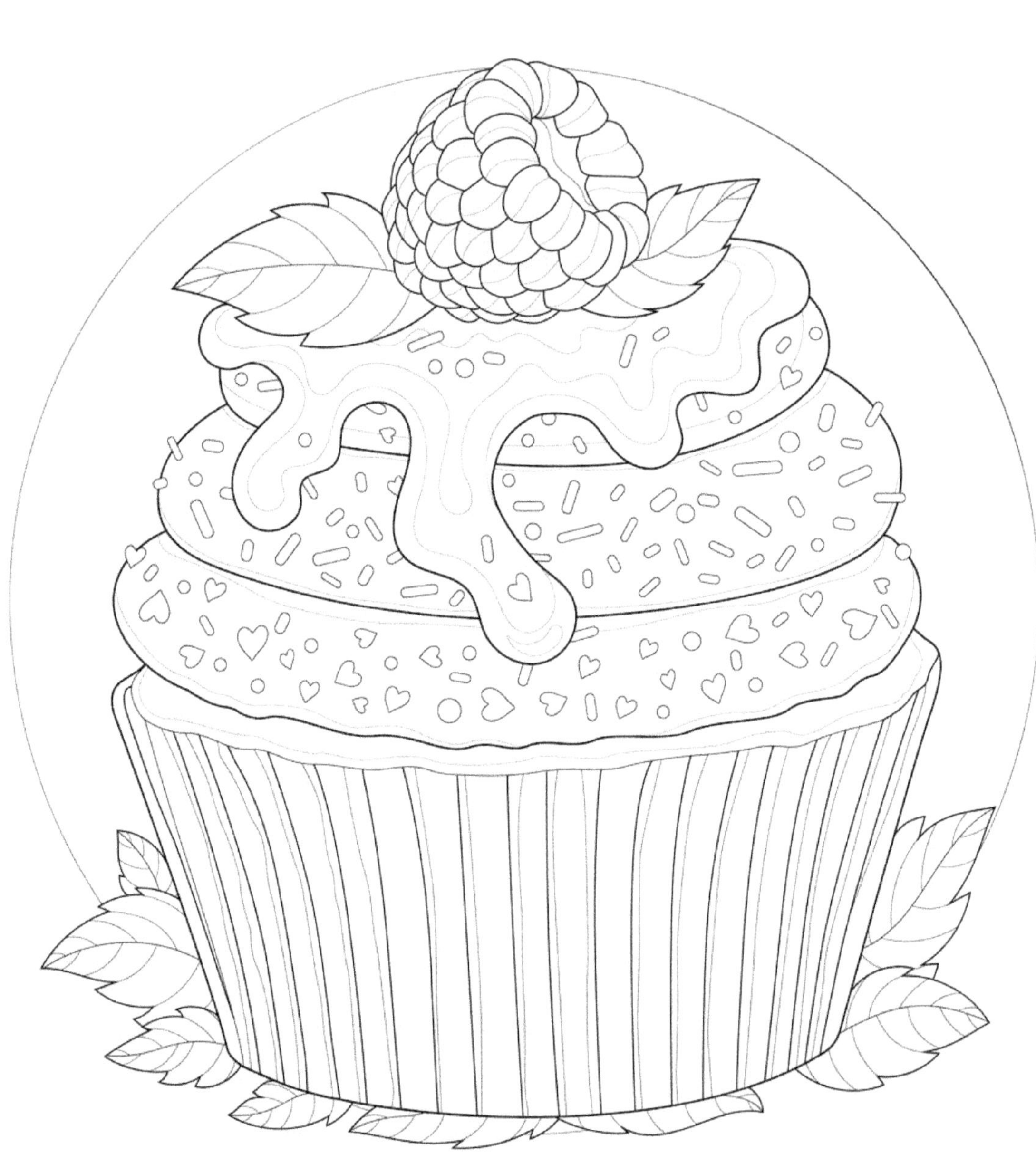

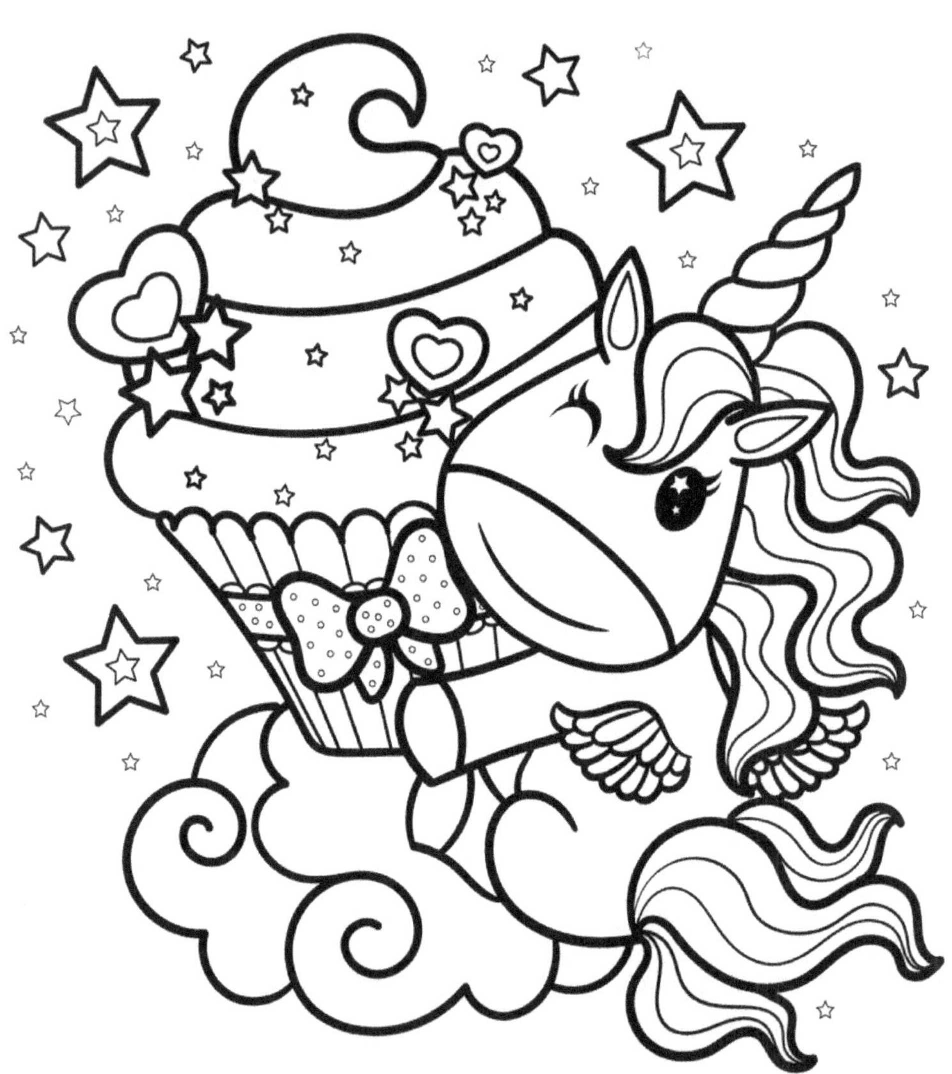

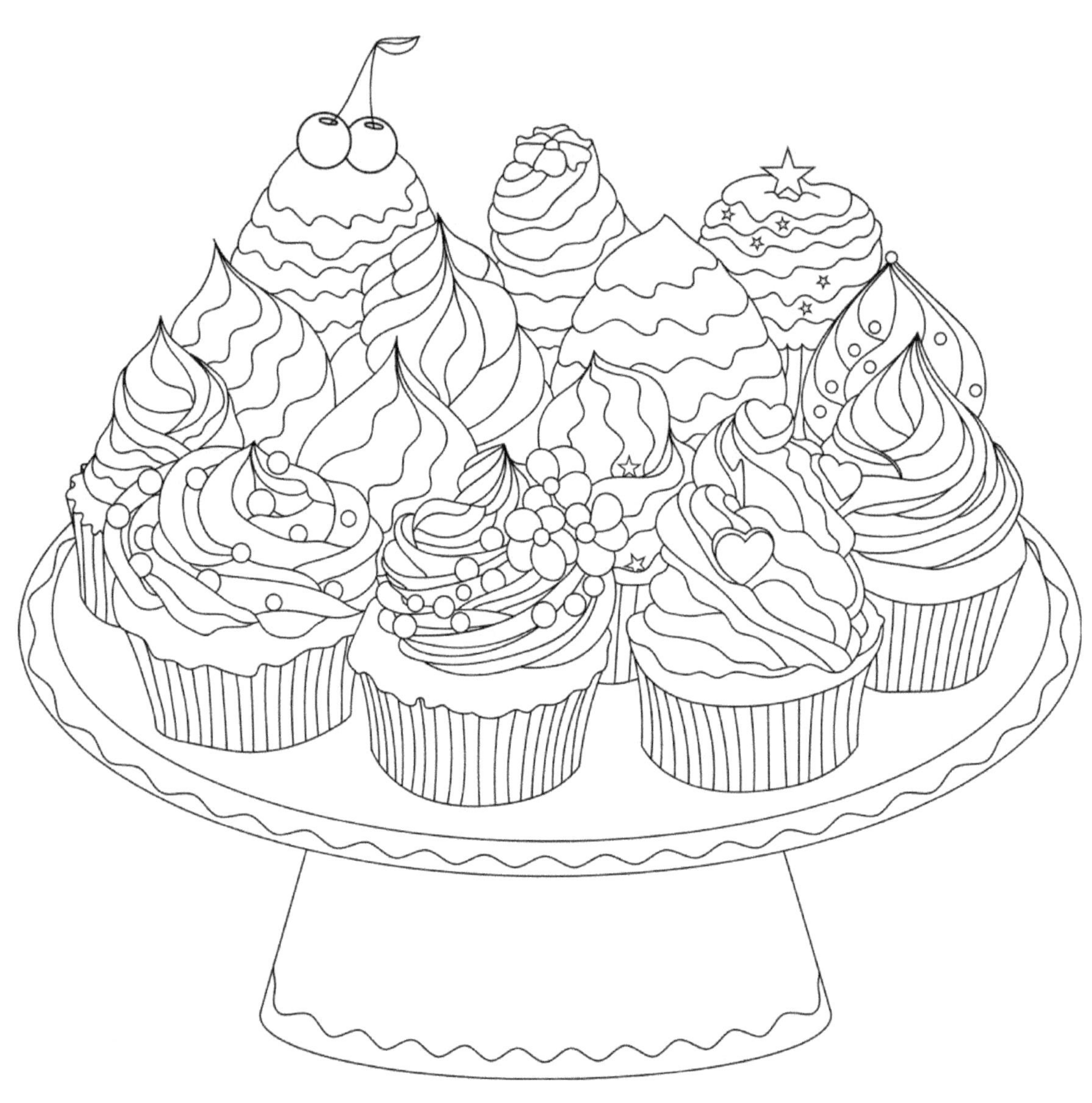

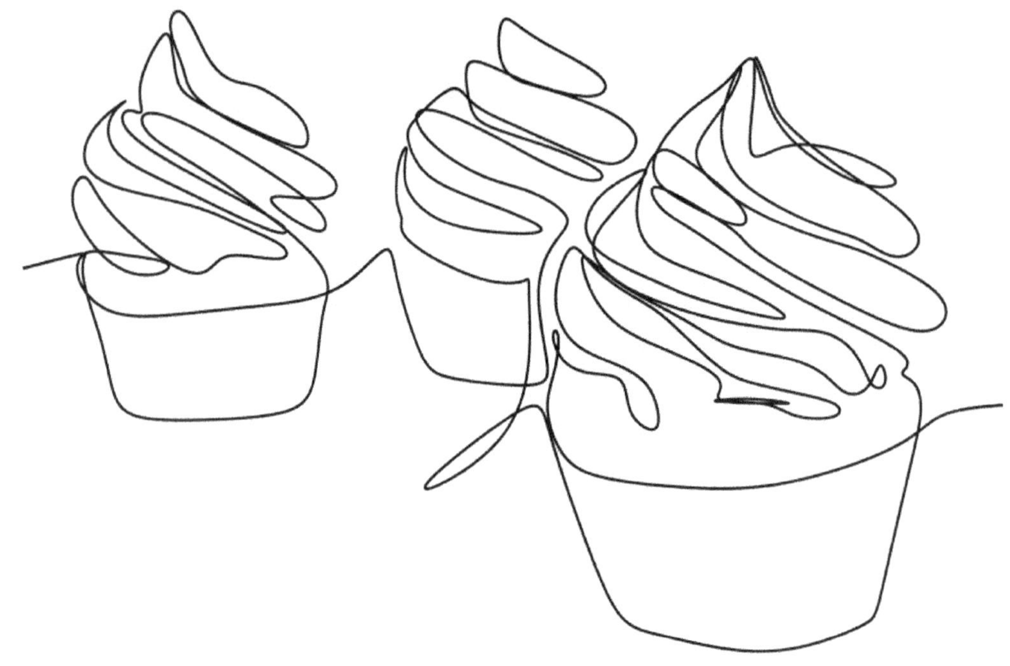

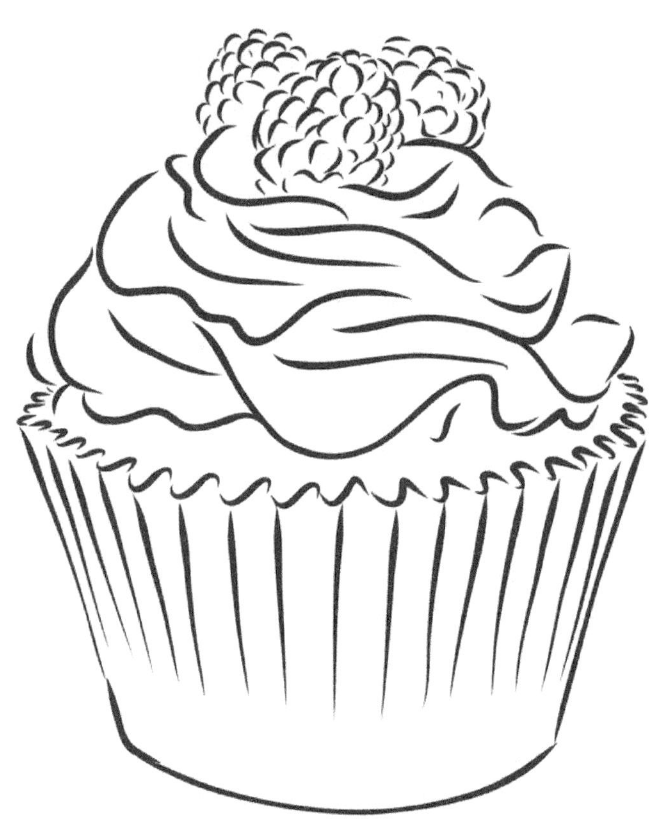

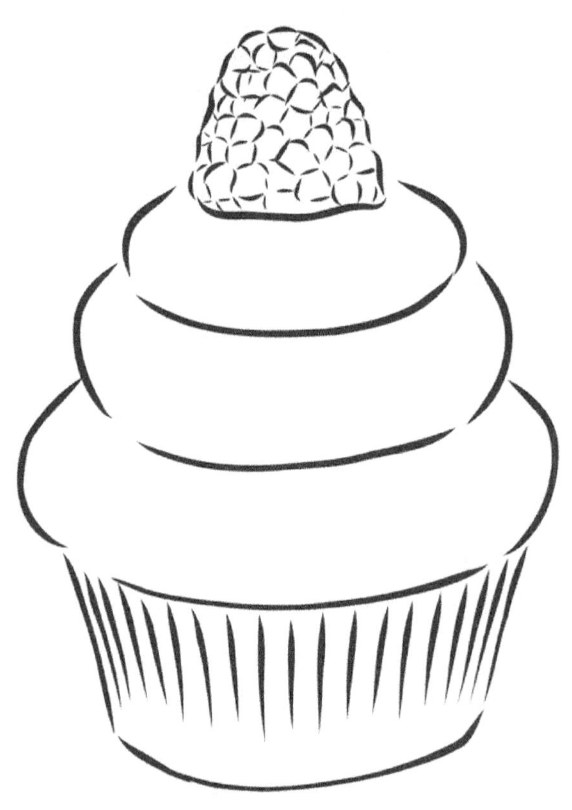

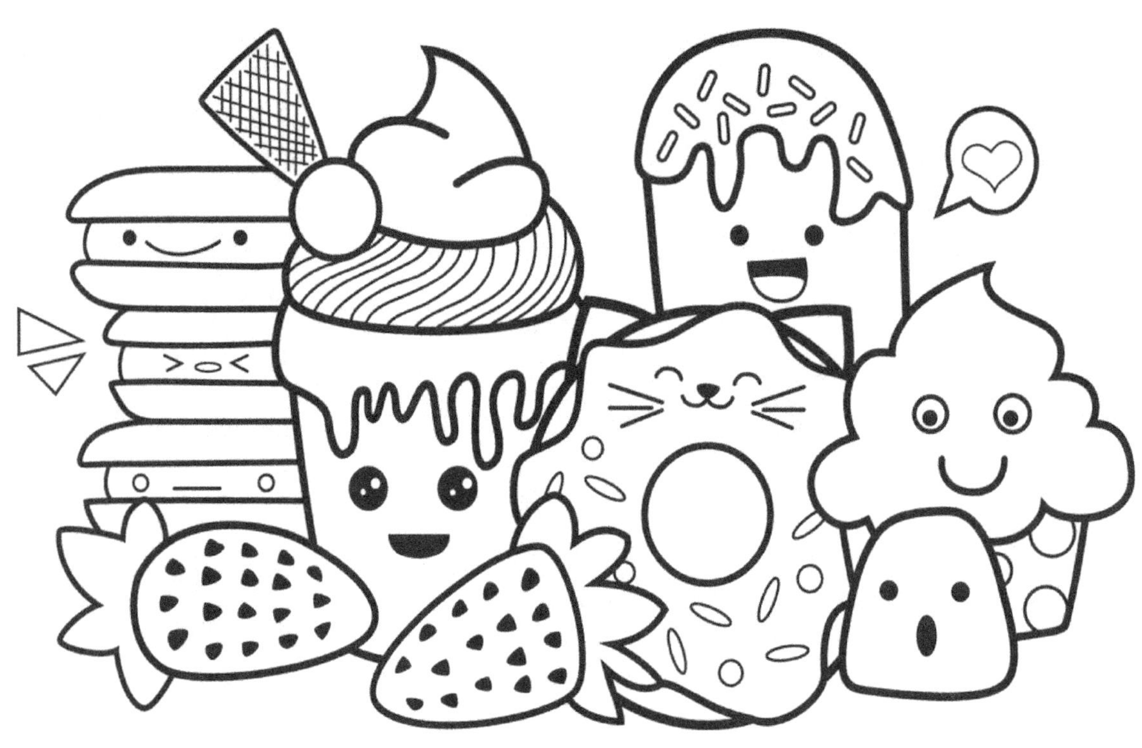

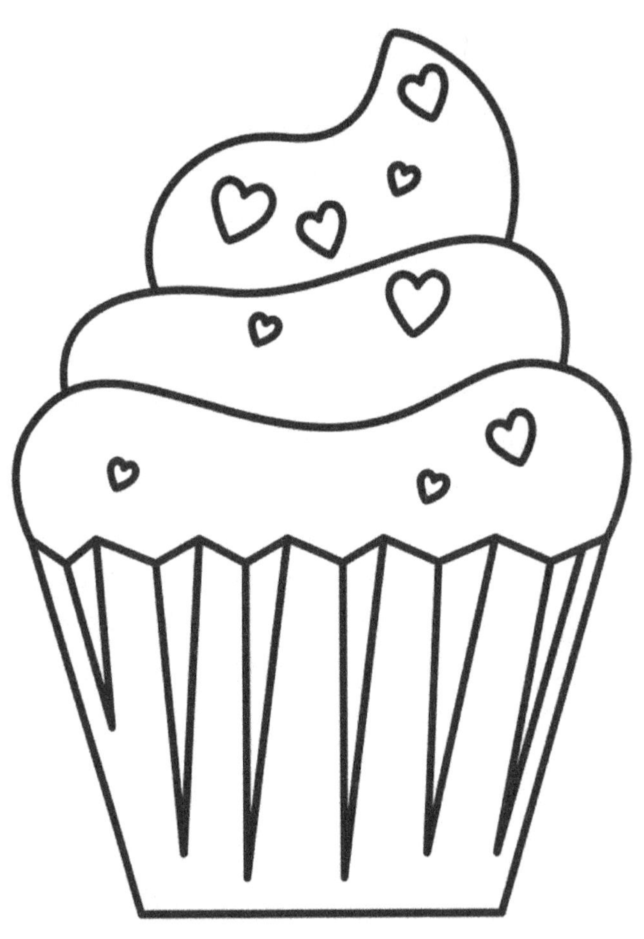

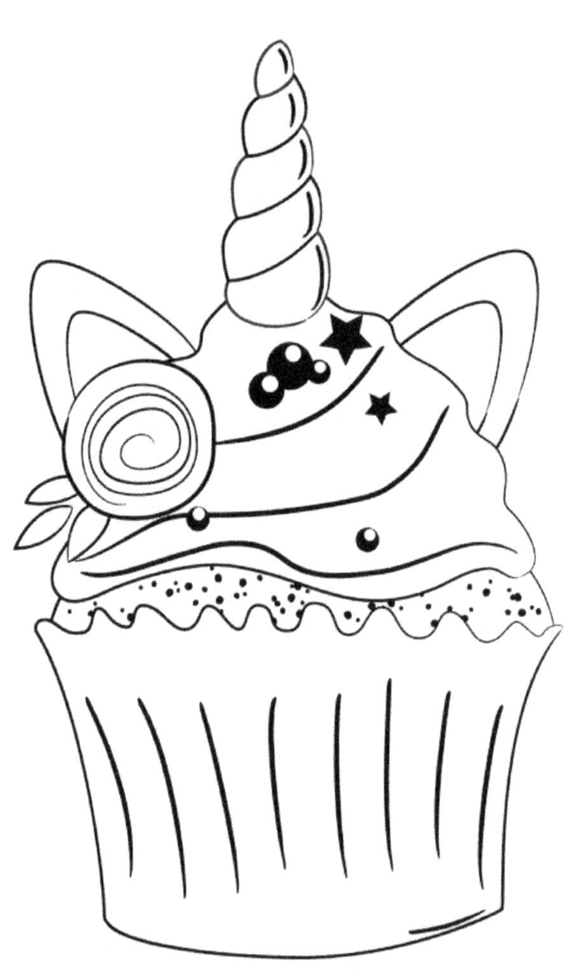

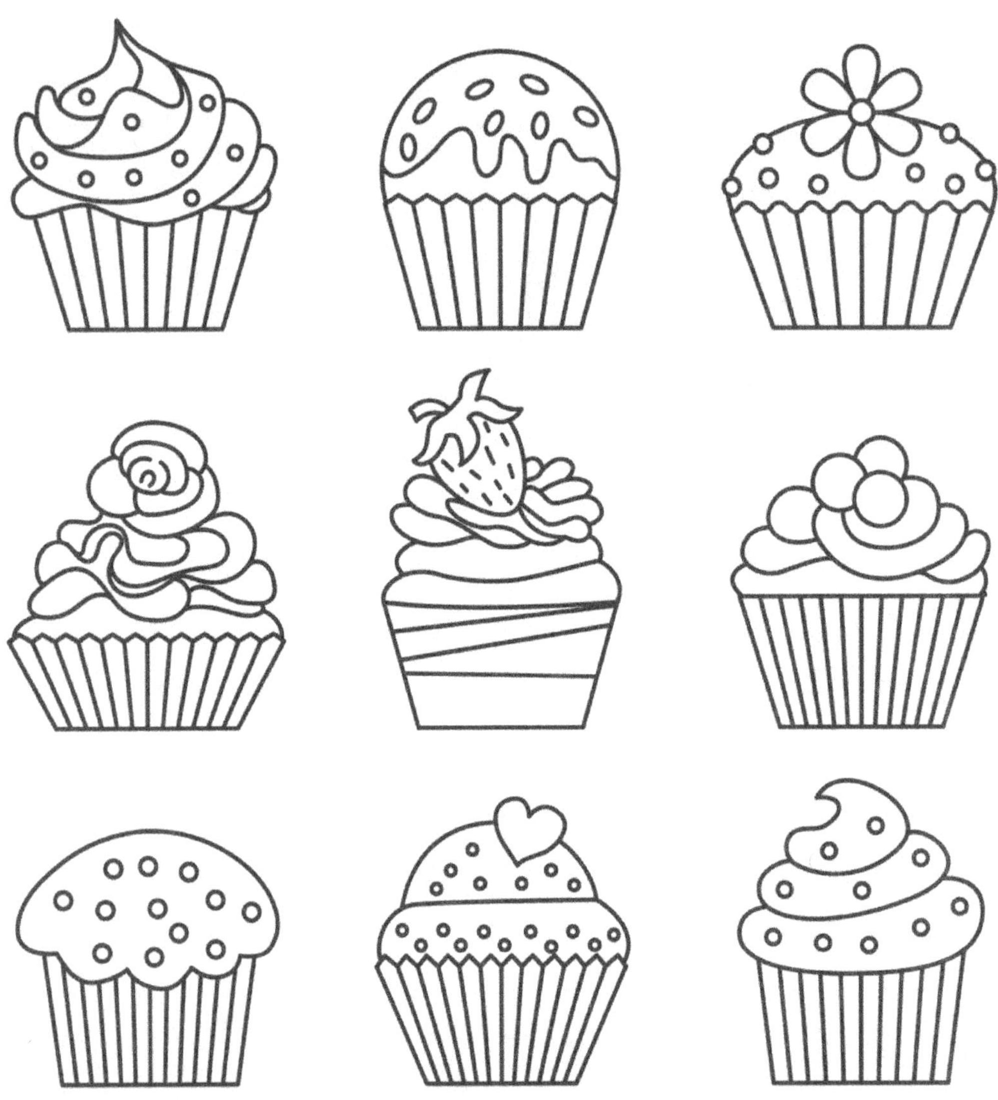

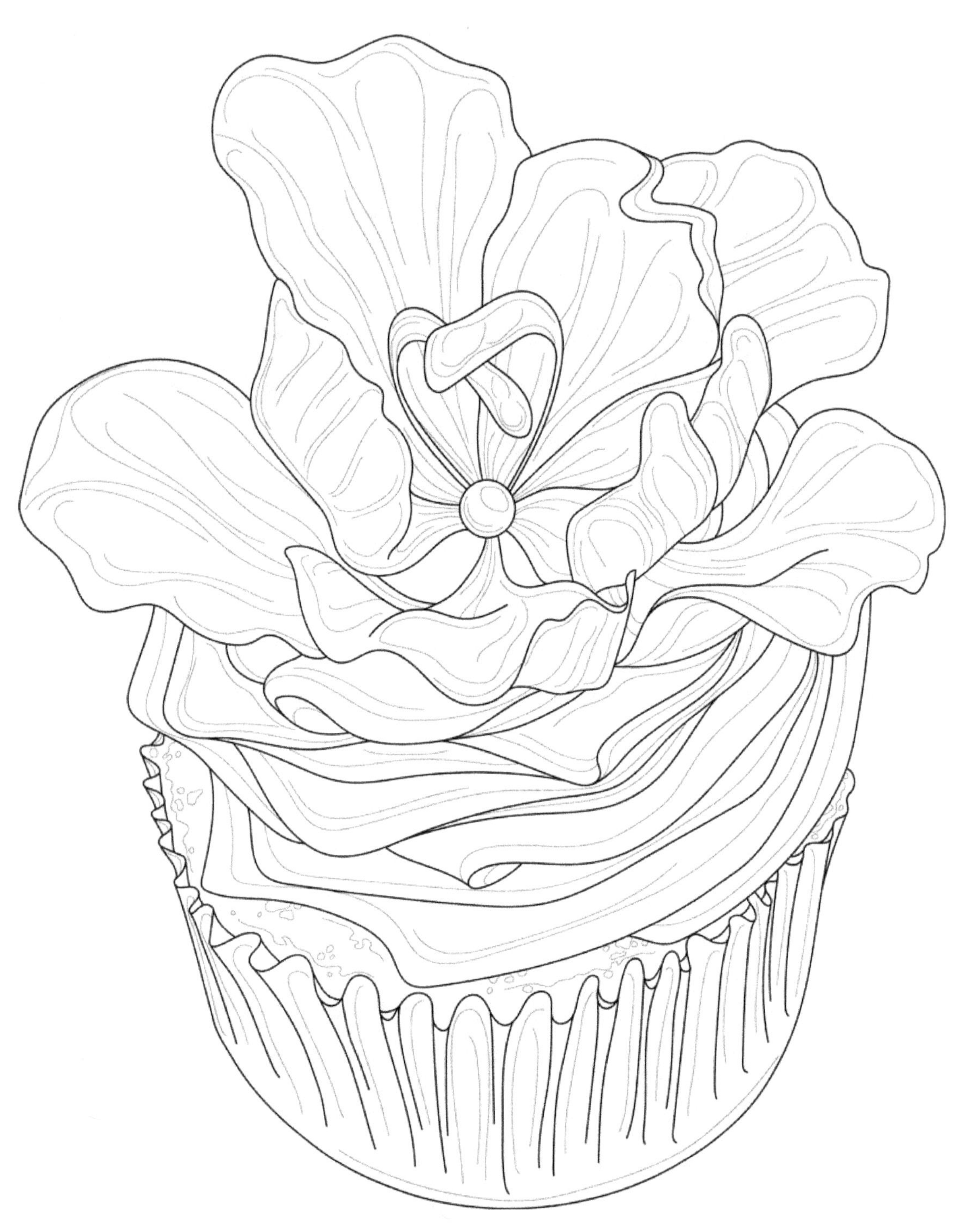

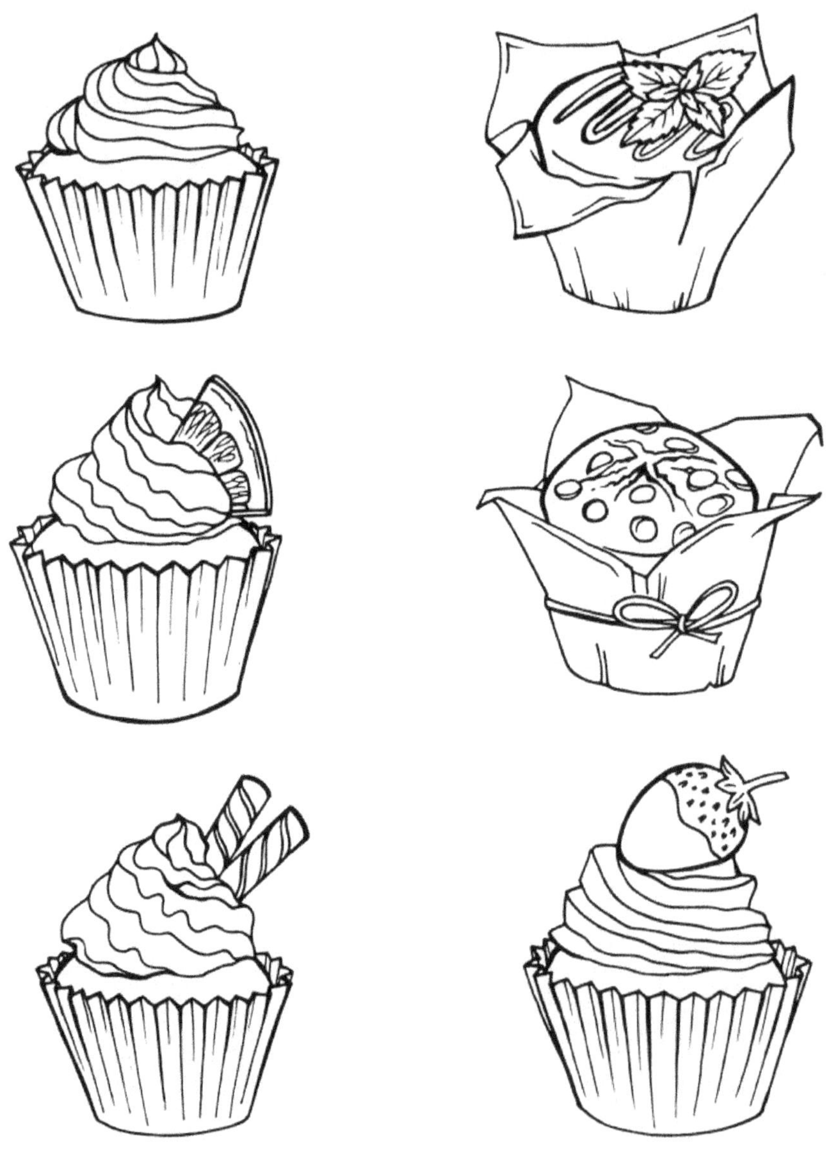

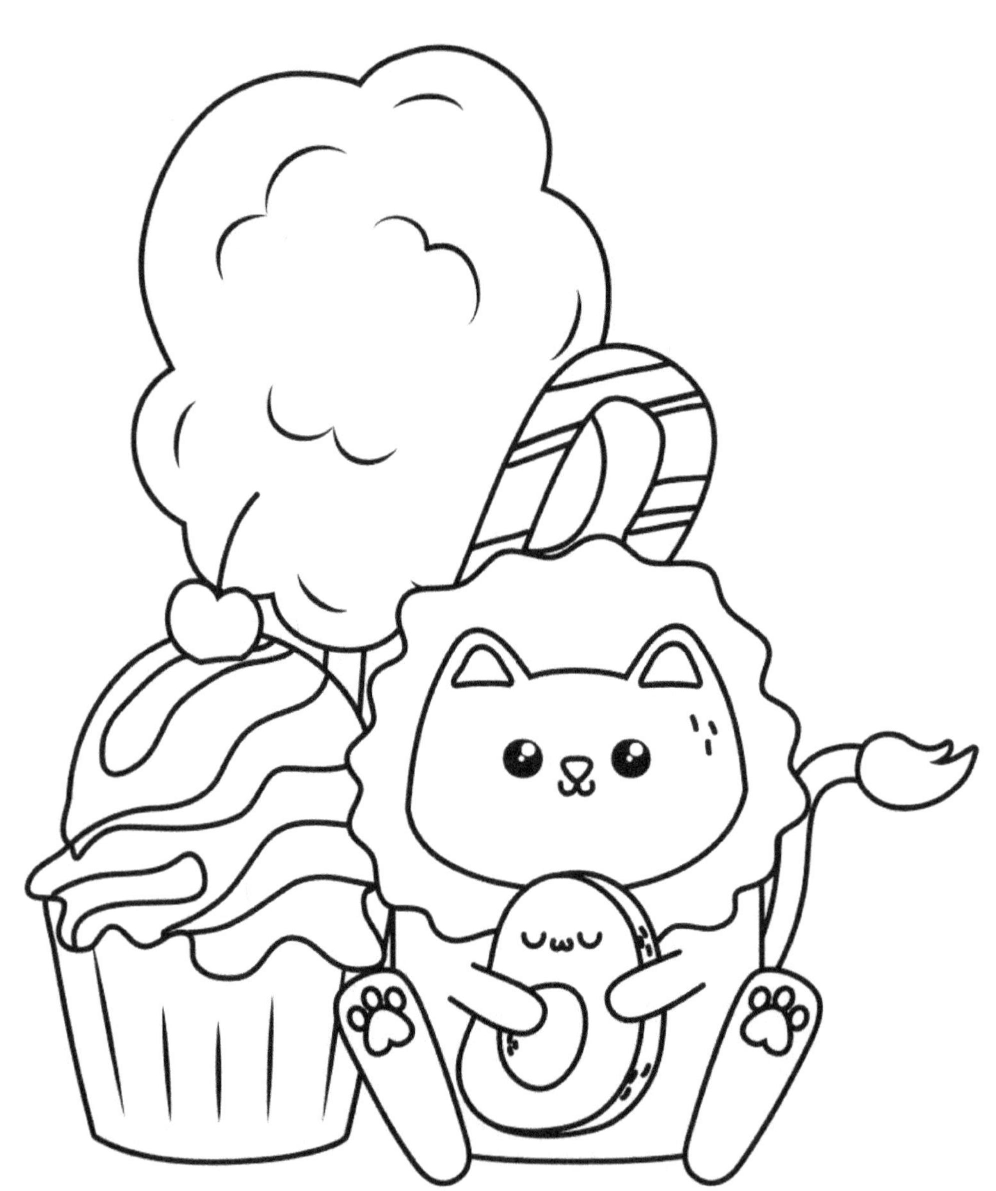

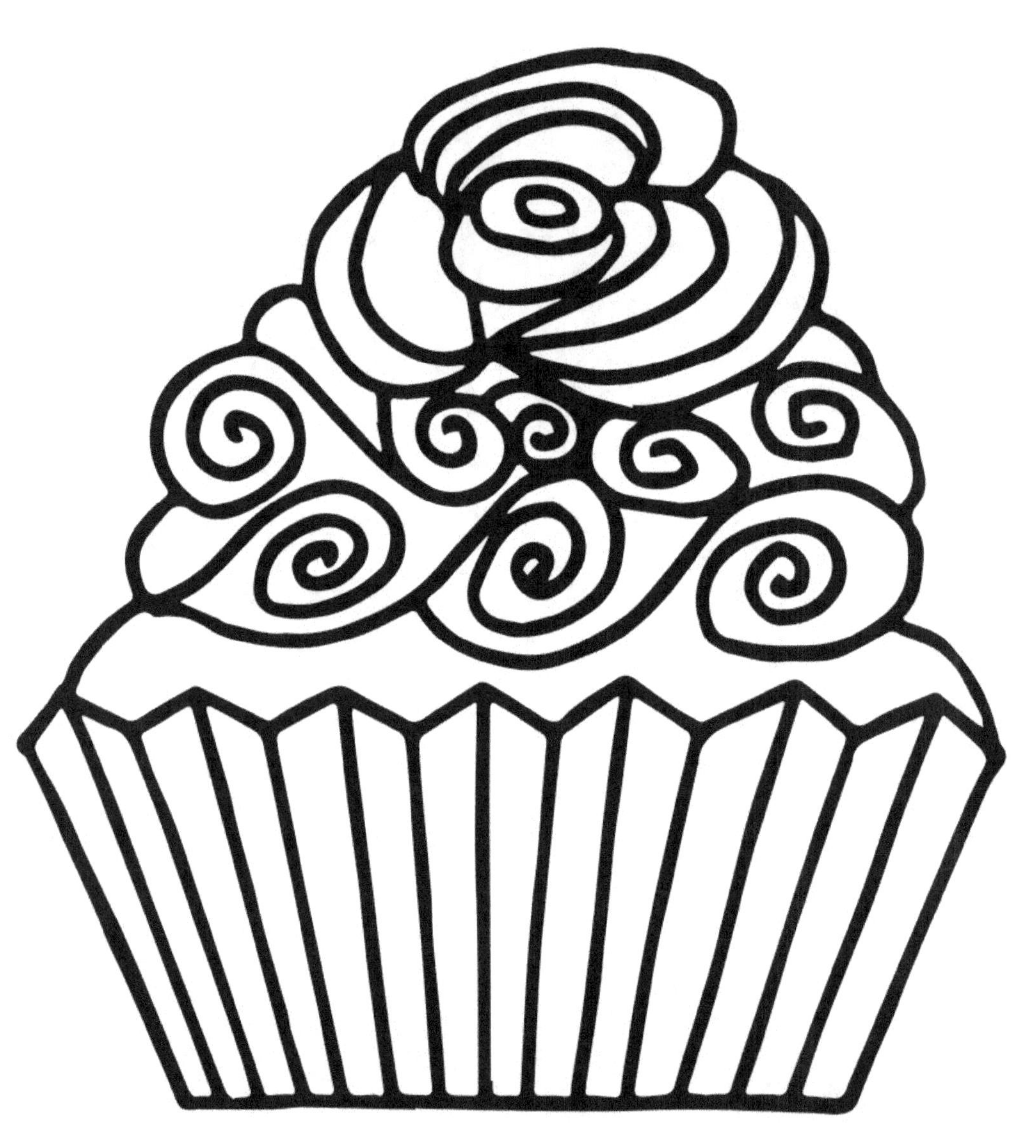

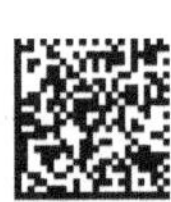
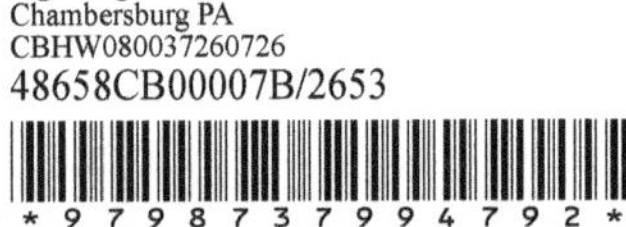